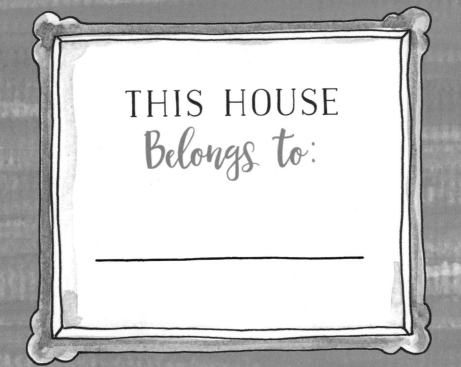

THIS HOUSE
Belongs to:

_____

THE DIY
Home Planner

KariAnne Wood

Illustrations by Michal Sparks

HARVEST HOUSE PUBLISHERS
EUGENE, OREGON

Scripture quotations are taken from the King James Version of the Bible.

Cover by Nicole Dougherty
Interior Design by Faceout Studio, Paul Nielsen

Published in association with William K. Jensen Literary Agency, 119 Bampton Court, Eugene, Oregon 97404.

The DIY Home Planner
Text copyright © 2018 KariAnne Wood
Photography copyright © 2018 KariAnne Wood
Artwork copyright © 2018 Michal Sparks
Various interior illustrated patterns © OGri/iStock, © Natalie Zakharov/Shutterstock, © IraChe/Shutterstock, © donatas1205/iStock, © malyshkamju/iStock, © Svetlomne/iStock, © Tasiania/iStock, © Olga_Aleksieieva/iStock, © Karma15381/iStock, © Any_Li/iStock, © Natouche/iStock, © tabuday/iStock, © AnnaDolzhenko/iStock
Published by Harvest House Publishers
Eugene, Oregon 97408
www.harvesthousepublishers.com

ISBN 978-0-7369-7177-5 (pbk.)

Library of Congress Cataloging-in-Publication Data

Names: Wood, KariAnne, author. | Sparks, Michal, illustrator.
Title: The DIY home planner / KariAnne Wood ; illustrations by Michal Sparks.
Description: Eugene, Oregon : Harvest House Publishers, 2018.
Identifiers: LCCN 2017027340 (print) | LCCN 2017027736 (ebook) | ISBN 9780736971782 (ebook) | ISBN 9780736971775 (pbk.)
Subjects: LCSH: Interior decoration--Amateurs' manuals.
Classification: LCC NK2115 (ebook) | LCC NK2115 .W8295 2018 (print) | DDC 747--dc23
LC record available at https://lccn.loc.gov/2017027340

Printed in China

17 18 19 20 21 22 23 24 25 26 / RDS-FO / 10 9 8 7 6 5 4 3 2 1

This book would never have been possible
without my mother. Thank you for...

my first Barbie house,

showing me that wallpaper scraps have endless possibilities,

all those miniature salt dough vegetables,

and living your faith so I could see.

I love you more.

KariAnne

TABLE OF
Contents

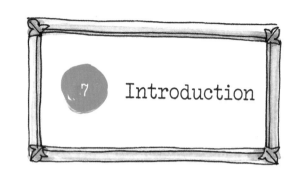

7 Introduction

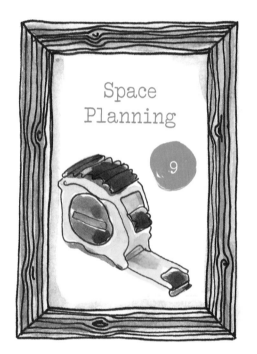

Space Planning

9

23 Paint Colors

37

Flooring Options

53

Wall Treatments

71 Window Treatments

85 Lighting Guide

97 Pattern Mixing

111 Accessory Styling

124 Conclusion & Resources

129 Extras

Introduction

I still remember the first day I fell in love with my house. It was early on a spring morning when the sun was shining and the birds were chirping and fluffy white clouds were floating by in a blue Kentucky sky. I poured a cup of coffee and walked from room to room—waking up the house along the way. I fluffed the pillows in the living room and told it how beautiful it was. I straightened the curtains in the dining room and reminded the dining room chairs they were amazing. I stacked bowls in the dishwasher and whispered softly to the kitchen that it was my favorite room in the entire world.

My house is loved; however, it isn't perfect. *Not even close.* But here's the thing...

...neither am I.

It took me a long time to figure out how to embrace the *me* that I am. I spent years trying to have the perfect house and the perfect me. I wasted so much time comparing my beginning to someone else's ending. I looked at the green grass on the other side of the fence and felt that my house was inadequate—that it was never going to be good enough. I wanted to click my ruby-red slippers together and transform my home and myself into someone taller and skinnier with perfect hair who could rock a prairie skirt, concho belt, and Lee Press-On Nails.

Check out the back of
the book for some
FUN EXTRAS
including a DIY for an
origami bookmark!

And then? One day I stopped comparing. I stopped hoping and wishing and planning and dreaming for something I wasn't and embraced the *me* that had been there all along. The *me* that was created by an incredible, amazing, awe-inspiring God who designed me with a plan and a purpose. I'm imperfect and distressed and worn around the edges with flaws and weaknesses, and I'm a sinner saved by grace. Every detail. Every line. Every flaw.

Every imperfection.

This is my prayer for you with this planner. I want it to inspire you. I want it to spark ideas. I want it to encourage you and uplift you and give you the tools you need to plan and design and decorate and create a space you love. Your home is one of a kind. Your home is loved. Your home is a reflection of who you are. And you, my friend, are perfect...

...just the way you are.

Space Planning

Planning your space is a lot like wearing Spanx to your high school reunion—it's absolutely necessary. Before you buy furniture, before you fall in love with a rug, before curtains are hung by the window with care, before a single candlestick takes up residence on the mantel, you need a plan.

Yikes!

I know, right? Planning? Who has time for a plan when you want to be shopping and dreaming and fluffing and styling? Take it from me and my school of decorating hard knocks—planning is the first step to making your space everything you want and so much more. It's the foundation to build your entire design on. A little planning can help with the overall arrangement for the room, prevent furniture heartbreak, and save you a few pennies (or hundreds of dollars) along the way.

DESIGN *life* LESSON

If you fail to plan...you plan to fail.

Take Measurements

Measure, measure...and then? Measure again. Start with the overall dimensions of the room. Measure the length, the width, and the height of the space. Then, using a pencil, mark these room dimensions on graph paper. Next, draw the lines of your room to scale on the paper and write down the length of each wall. These measurements will help you determine if your furniture will fit. In addition, make sure to record each of these measurements on page 16. That way you have a record of all your room dimensions for future projects.

 NOTE

This planner has several amazing tools to help you get started. We've created customized room planning pages (see pages 16 to 21) that will help you as you work through each of these steps. In addition, flip to page 135 for some standard-size furniture pieces you can cut out and move around before you move a single piece of anything into the space.

Mark Features

Before you start adding furniture, it's important to note on the space plan what is permanent to a space. On the graph paper, mark the electrical outlets, light switches, windows, and doors in the space. In addition, make sure to include any permanent fixtures in the room, such as pillars, fireplaces, closets, and built-ins.

Anchor the Room

Now you are ready to start moving your miniature furniture pieces around the outlines of the room you have penciled on your graph paper.

Begin with your largest piece of furniture.

In living rooms, this would typically be the couch or sectional; in dining rooms, it's the dining table; in bedrooms, it's the bed. This is the anchor piece for your design.

 TIP

Many times, with larger pieces such as couches and beds, you want the piece to face the entrance to the space.

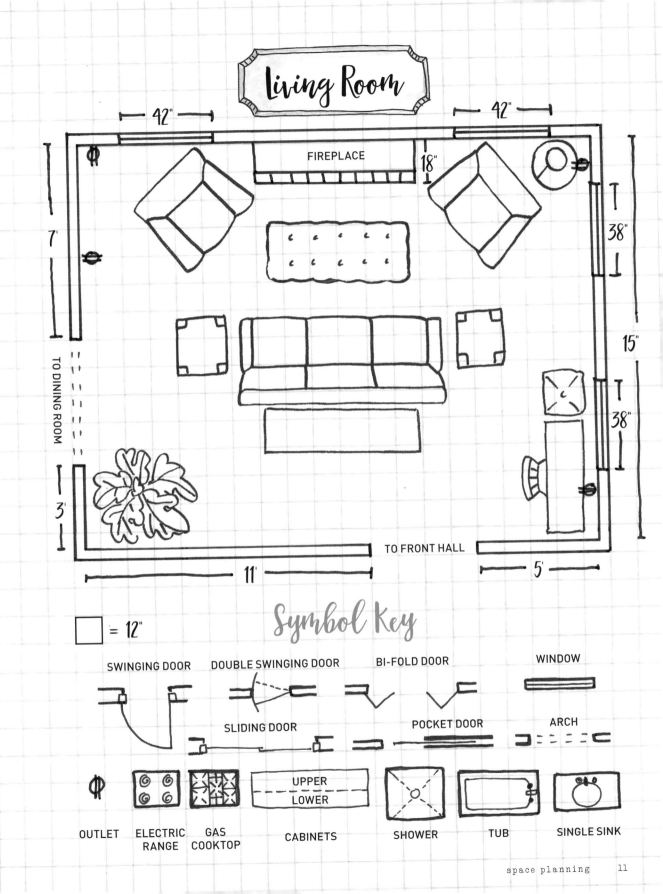

Living Room

FIREPLACE

42"   42"   18"   7'   38"   15"   38"   3'

TO DINING ROOM

TO FRONT HALL

11'   5'

Symbol Key

☐ = 12"

SWINGING DOOR	DOUBLE SWINGING DOOR	BI-FOLD DOOR	WINDOW
	SLIDING DOOR	POCKET DOOR	ARCH

UPPER
LOWER

OUTLET   ELECTRIC RANGE   GAS COOKTOP   CABINETS   SHOWER   TUB   SINGLE SINK

Arrange Your Furniture

Now that your anchor piece is set, add in chairs, sofa tables, coffee tables, rugs, lamps, hutches, and accent pieces to the space. This bird's-eye view of the room will help you see the orientation of different pieces of furniture to each other.

Place furniture slightly away from walls. For example, add a sofa table behind the back of the couch, or angle chairs to create a conversation area instead of lining them up against the wall. Bring your furniture into the space, and the room will instantly feel more welcoming.

Design for comfort. Place tables within easy reach of seating to accommodate drinks. Make sure there are three points of lighting in separate areas of each space to warm up the room. Tuck ottomans and poufs under tables for extra seating. Add oversized baskets next to chairs to store throws and additional pillows.

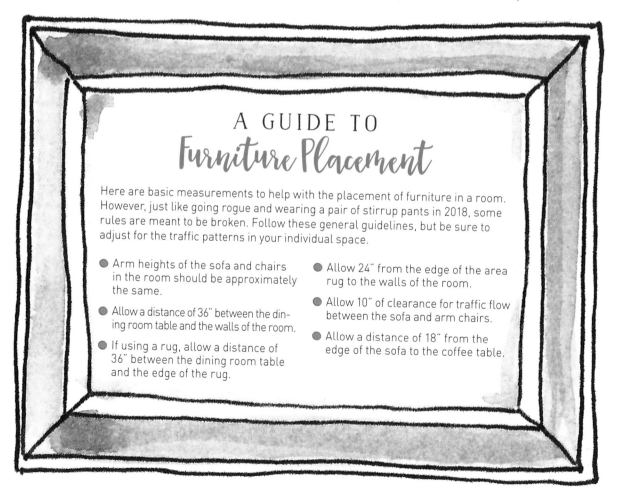

A GUIDE TO
Furniture Placement

Here are basic measurements to help with the placement of furniture in a room. However, just like going rogue and wearing a pair of stirrup pants in 2018, some rules are meant to be broken. Follow these general guidelines, but be sure to adjust for the traffic patterns in your individual space.

- Arm heights of the sofa and chairs in the room should be approximately the same.

- Allow a distance of 36" between the dining room table and the walls of the room.

- If using a rug, allow a distance of 36" between the dining room table and the edge of the rug.

- Allow 24" from the edge of the area rug to the walls of the room.

- Allow 10" of clearance for traffic flow between the sofa and arm chairs.

- Allow a distance of 18" from the edge of the sofa to the coffee table.

Add a Rug

Once your room design is completed, you can determine the size of rug you need for the space. Ideally, the legs of the furniture should touch the rug, and there should be approximately 18" of floor between the rug and the wall. In a dining room, the chairs and table should be located on the area rug. Draw in the size of rug needed for the space on the plan.

Can you believe it? You've done it!

You are an official design rock star.

You and your space plan and your furniture are ready to party like champions and take on the next steps in designing your space.

 TIP

In a larger room, rugs help to establish zones in a space. For example, create a dining area in one part of the space and a seating area in another. An easy way to define spaces in the room is with area rugs.

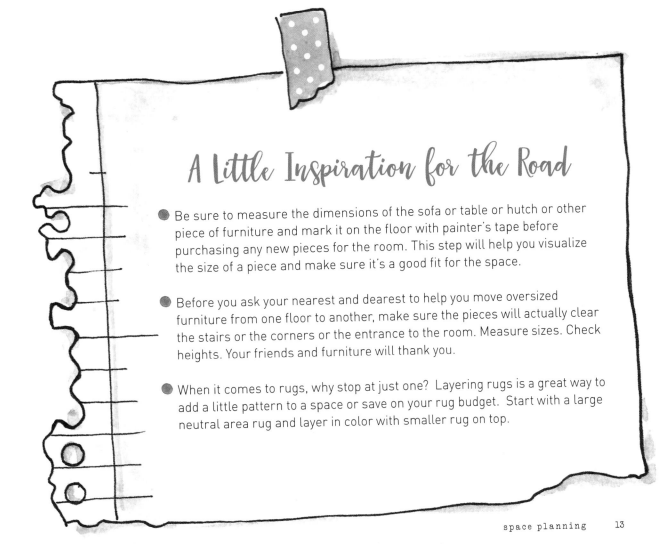

A Little Inspiration for the Road

● Be sure to measure the dimensions of the sofa or table or hutch or other piece of furniture and mark it on the floor with painter's tape before purchasing any new pieces for the room. This step will help you visualize the size of a piece and make sure it's a good fit for the space.

● Before you ask your nearest and dearest to help you move oversized furniture from one floor to another, make sure the pieces will actually clear the stairs or the corners or the entrance to the room. Measure sizes. Check heights. Your friends and furniture will thank you.

● When it comes to rugs, why stop at just one? Layering rugs is a great way to add a little pattern to a space or save on your rug budget. Start with a large neutral area rug and layer in color with smaller rug on top.

Check your measurements

Measure your couch height

Layer in a rug

Add
layers
for
comfort

RECORD YOUR ROOM & ITS MEASUREMENTS

LENGTH   WIDTH   HEIGHT

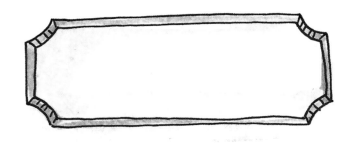

LENGTH　　　　WIDTH　　　　HEIGHT

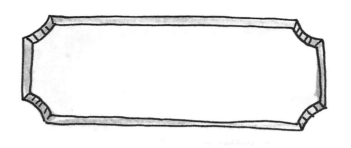

....

LENGTH   WIDTH   HEIGHT

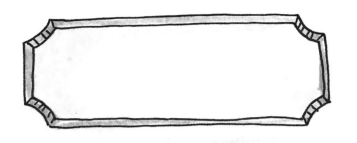

LENGTH   WIDTH   HEIGHT

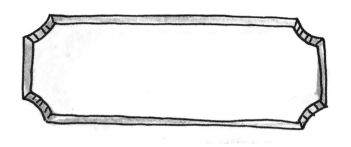

LENGTH   WIDTH   HEIGHT

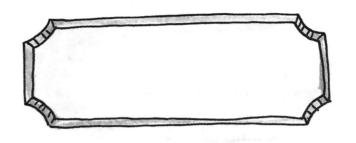

LENGTH · WIDTH · HEIGHT

Paint color can be a tricky thing. One minute you are best friends, and the next minute you want to break up and act as though you've never met. I get it. After all, I'm the girl who painted my living room four times before I found a paint color I'd want to hang out with for more than five minutes. The key to finding the right color for your walls is a combination of a little knowledge, a few paint-picking tips, and an extra helping of luck.

Here are some of my favorite tried-and-true tips to help with your next paint color decision.

DESIGN *Life* LESSON

Always remember to show that paint can who's boss.

A GUIDE TO
Painting Terms

In case you want to sound extra paint-smart, here are a few of my favorite terms:

DRY BRUSH—A painting technique used to create a cross-hatch pattern with a dry brush dipped lightly in paint.

DRY TO RECOAT—The stage of drying when the next coat can be applied.

FAUX BOIS—A paint treatment that mimics the look of wood grain.

GLAZE—A medium mixed with paint used to create faux finishes.

HUE—A color or shade.

PRIMER—A product applied as a first layer to help prepare the surface for painting.

SATURATION—The intensity of the color; the visual strength of a surface color.

SHEEN—A soft luster on the surface.

TROMPE L'OEIL—Painting designed to recreate the look of a three-dimensional object.

Choose Your Paint Color Last

 NOTE

Check out page 100 for tips on how to create a cohesive color palette.

Have you ever found the perfect pair of earrings in the most beautiful color you've ever seen, and you brought them home and then spent hours trying to plan an outfit to coordinate with them? That is so much harder than it looks. It's a lot like picking a shade of paint before you've selected the furnishings for the room.

Let your furniture do the talking.

Listen to your sofa or your rug or your curtains. They all know what's up. Select a color you like from the pattern on a statement piece in your space. Even if you don't match the color exactly, the existing pieces of furniture set a warm or cool tone for the room and help determine paint selection. Choosing the paint last makes the whole process easier.

Trust me. It's a lot less expensive to buy a new can of paint than a new sofa.

Make Friends with Your Paint Strip

The paint strip is the first step in your painting journey—where paint goes all Julie Andrews and starts at the very beginning. Visit your local paint store, spend a few minutes in front of those giant stands of paint strips, and choose a few selections you'd like to take home. Or maybe more than a few—maybe a dozen or more. This is the time to let your fingers do the dreaming.

Just remember that the darkest color on the paint strip is there to help.

When you are looking at colors on the dozens of paint strips you've selected from the store and tucked into this journal, many times the colors will appear to be the same. THEY ARE NOT. Do not be fooled. It's easy to discard a color at first glance, but instead hold firm, resist temptation, and look at the darkest color at the bottom of the paint strip.

The reason? Each of these paint color families are tinted differently. For example, a khaki can have a pink base or a blue base. A gray can have a green base or a brown base. A red can have an orange base or a pink base. One of the easiest ways to determine the true color of the paint is to start with the darkest color on the strip. This color has the most color saturation and, therefore, helps showcase the actual colors on the strip.

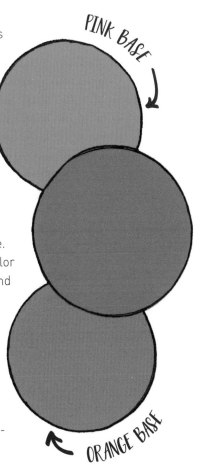

PINK BASE

ORANGE BASE

Consider the Surface

The same paint color does not look the same on all surfaces. I know, right? Who knew? I'm as amazed as you are. Lighting in a space can make a big difference too, but a surface is equally important.

Here's an easy guide to help determine what adjustments to make when painting a space based on where you are painting:

CEILING

When painting your ceiling any other color than white, go at least one shade lighter. Color on a ceiling appears darker than on a wall.

FLOORS

When choosing a color for the floor, you might want to go one shade darker than the original paint color. Color on the floor appears lighter than on a wall.

FINISH

Different paint finishes can make the paint look lighter or darker. For example, flat paint absorbs light due to its chalky finish and sometimes appears lighter. In contrast, glossy finishes can make the paint appear slightly darker.

MOLDINGS

If your moldings are painted white, hold the paint chip up next to the molding when selecting the paint color. This allows you to see the color relationship between your molding and your paint.

You really want them all to get along.

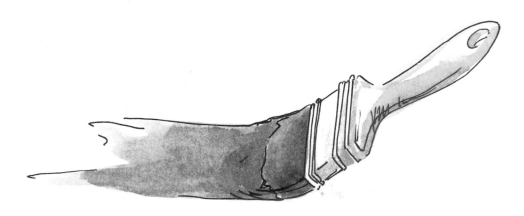

A GUIDE TO
Paint Sheens

You have your paint color. You are officially paint-mazing. Pat yourself on the back and select a sheen. Here's a quick guide to selecting the perfect paint sheen for your project:

FLAT—This paint sheen lacks any finish or shine. Paint can almost appear to be chalky. Many times, flat paint is used on ceilings to absorb light.

EGGSHELL—This paint sheen has slightly more finish than flat but less than satin. It's a great choice to hide imperfections on the wall.

SATIN—Excellent choice for most walls. It has a soft, warm luster that slightly reflects light, but it doesn't have too much of a shine.

SEMIGLOSS—Used for trim or doors, this paint has a glossy sheen without too much shine.

GLOSS—This paint sheen has the highest level of shine and is the most durable. It's a great choice for kitchens, bathrooms, or other high traffic areas.

Remember That Saturation Is Key

If you could only take one tip away from this section, please remember this piece of completely unsolicited advice when you are standing in front of that giant paint display. Find the color you want. And then?

Go one shade darker.

I know. It's scary. It's only natural that we tend to go a little lighter with our paint choices. The challenge is that natural light and room angles and corners and spaces and ceiling height can wash out a color and make it appear lighter than on the paint chip. It might seem counterintuitive, but most of the time you might be happier with a little more saturation.

It's also important to take the overall space into consideration when considering saturation. Let your room dictate the amount of color you need. For example, if the room has sunbeams of natural light bouncing off the walls, you'll want to compensate with a slightly darker color saturation. Or, if your space doesn't have windows or other sources of light, too much saturation may become a little overwhelming.

Sample, Sample, Sample

After you have studied your paint chips, held them up to your molding, and determined which surfaces you want to paint, limit your color choices to three.

Or four if you are feeling extra paint-venturous.

Then return to the paint store and buy a small sample of each of the paint selections. Spring for the paint sample. Don't take a shortcut with just the paint chips. You are so close. You're almost there. The finish line is just around the corner. Don't let the cost of a sample come between you and the perfect wall color.

It's a fact. A painted swatch on the wall is better than the color on a paint chip every day of the week.

Paint the samples on the wall and live with them for a few days. Study them during the morning, walk past them in the afternoon, and look at them again at night. Look at the color on a cloudy day and again when sunlight streams into the space. After you've spent some time getting to know your paint samples a little better, figure out which one works best for your space.

Then ask it to be your BFFAW. (That's *best friends for a while* in paint speak).

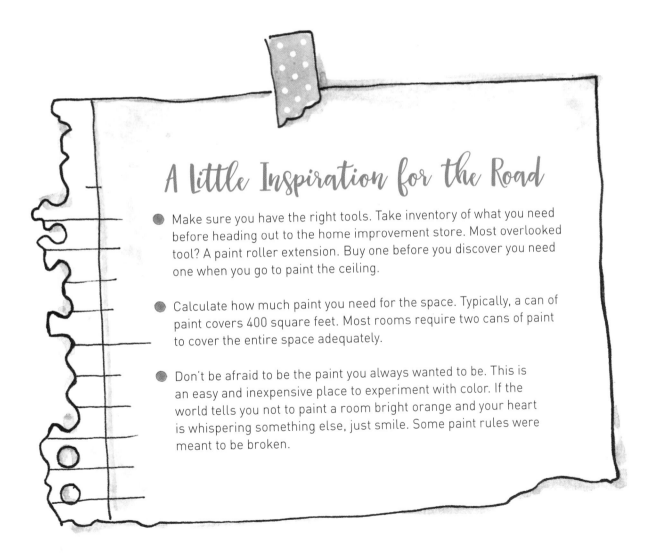

A Little Inspiration for the Road

- Make sure you have the right tools. Take inventory of what you need before heading out to the home improvement store. Most overlooked tool? A paint roller extension. Buy one before you discover you need one when you go to paint the ceiling.

- Calculate how much paint you need for the space. Typically, a can of paint covers 400 square feet. Most rooms require two cans of paint to cover the entire space adequately.

- Don't be afraid to be the paint you always wanted to be. This is an easy and inexpensive place to experiment with color. If the world tells you not to paint a room bright orange and your heart is whispering something else, just smile. Some paint rules were meant to be broken.

Choose a
bold wall
color

Paint
a fun
pattern

Try a
timeless
neutral

Let your rug start the story

RECORD YOUR PAINT
COLORS ROOM BY ROOM

Bedroom

FILL IN YOUR
PAINT COLORS
OR PASTE THE
SWATCHES HERE

WALLS   **CEILINGS**   **MOLDINGS**   **DOORS**

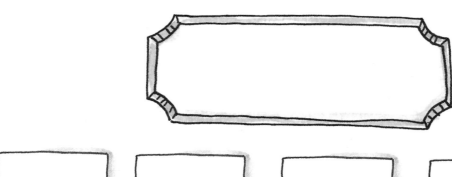

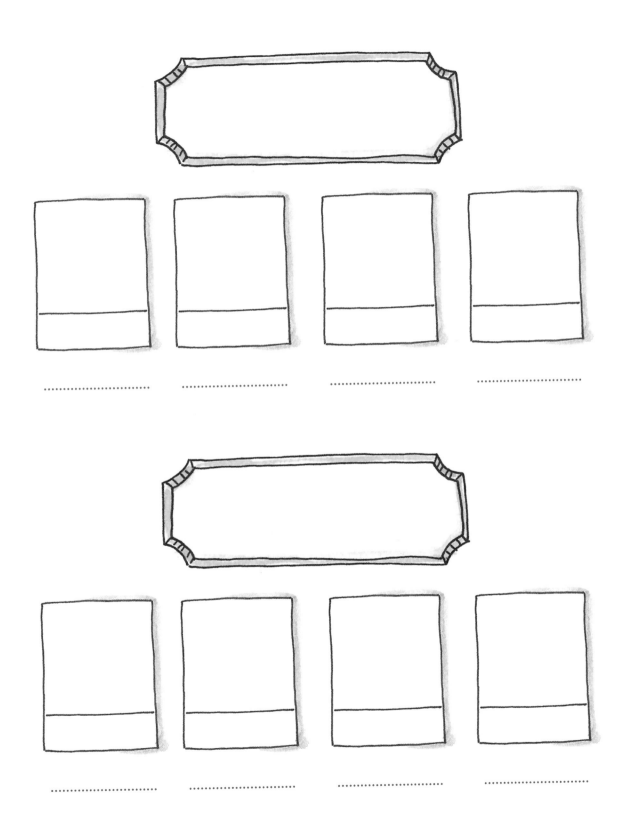

Flooring Options

C an I tell you a secret? I've written poems to my floors before. I know, right? Sonnets and odes and limericks and couplets and even the occasional haiku.

I can't help it. A really good flooring choice moves me to iambic pentameter.

Poetry aside, it's important to understand that flooring is the foundation of the design of any space. Typically, it's one of the most expensive design elements in a room and often the hardest to change. You can move a couch in and out of a space. You can paint the walls five times. You can change your curtains to roman shades in a weekend.

But the floor? It takes up permanent residence.

Knowledge is flooring power. Educating yourself on available flooring options is the best place to start when choosing flooring for a space. Among other things, it's important to evaluate cost, how easy a floor is to clean, and how easy the flooring material is to install.

Sometimes it seems as though there are enough varieties of flooring to fill the Smithsonian. Here's a look at a few of the basic categories of flooring choices.

DESIGN *Life* LESSON

When taking that first step, make sure it's on flooring that speaks to your heart.

HELPFUL
Flooring Terms

Here's an easy reference guide on flooring:

BERBER—Carpet woven with small loops; traditionally flecked with different colors.

CHEVRON—A repeating pattern meeting at a sharp point that forms a V.

CORK—A type of flooring made from cork oak.

ENGINEERED WOOD—A wood product made by combining smaller particles with adhesives to form a composite material.

GROUT—A mix used to fill in tile joints; comes in a variety of colors.

GROUT SEALER—A sealant liquid used to help waterproof grout.

HAND-SCRAPED WOOD FLOORS—Floors scraped and distressed to create the look of vintage wood.

HERRINGBONE PATTERN—An arrangement of planks of wood in diagonal layers.

PEEL AND STICK TILE—Vinyl tile squares with a peel-off backing and an adhesive that adheres directly to the floor.

PILE—Refers to the density of fibers in a rug.

SHAG—Carpet with a deep pile, giving it a shaggy appearance.

SEAMS—The juncture where two pieces of flooring meet.

SUBFLOOR—The initial layer of flooring used as a foundation for additional flooring layers.

Hardwood

Hardwood is one of the most popular and sustainable flooring options on the market today. Current trends with hardwood include hand-scraped flooring, inlaid patterns, herringbone, and reclaimed wood.

PROS	CONS
• durable	• expensive
• natural element adds authenticity to a space	• requires professional installation
• easy to clean	• allows sound to bounce off the surface, creating an echo

 TIP

One of the most often-asked questions about hardwood flooring is: In what direction should the individual wood planks be installed? That's easy. Think of your house like a bowling alley without the pins. Lay the wood with one end facing the front door and one end facing the back, and you've answered the question. In other words, the wood should be laid perpendicular to the front of the house.

Laminate

Laminate is an affordable flooring option and serves as a great alternative to traditional choices, such as hardwood or brick. Current trends with laminate include reclaimed wood-look laminate, hand-scraped wood-look laminate, and wide plank laminate floors.

TIP

Laminate flooring isn't just for straight lines anymore. Why not get creative and add a pattern to your floor instead? Chevron and herringbone patterns work well with most types of laminate planks.

PROS	CONS
• easy to install	• cannot be sanded or refinished
• easy to clean	• surface texture tends to be smooth, lacking in depth
• inexpensive	• shows dust and dirt
• available in a wide variety of products mimicking higher-end flooring choices	

Bamboo

This eco-friendly flooring option has risen in popularity over the last ten years. Bamboo is one of the hardest floor surfaces available today, making it extremely durable.

PROS	CONS
• sustainable, long lasting	• susceptible to sunlight and can fade significantly
• easy to install	• can scratch easily
• easy to clean	• planks can shrink in locations with high humidity
• adds visual integrity to a space	

● TIP

Because of its distinctive look, bamboo is at home in a modern, contemporary setting. The lines of the flooring mimic modern furniture style with its angles and smooth finishes. Bamboo also works well with the modern country aesthetic.

Brick

As a traditional flooring material, brick floors offer a classic design from centuries past. Current trends include unusual brick patterns, such as chevron and herringbone, and lighter brick color options, such as whitewashed brick.

TIP

A little brick can go a long way. Brick flooring often works best in a single room due to the expense and the challenge of keeping it clean. Visually, it pairs well with classic traditional styling as well as a farmhouse design plan.

PROS	CONS
• durable	• expensive
• adds character and personality	• requires professional installation
• help to anchor the design of the room	• mortar can chip and stain
	• absorbs dirt

RUNNING BOND

BASKET WEAVE

HERRINGBONE

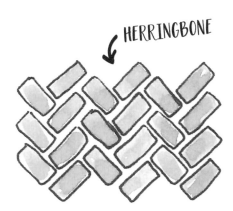

Tile

This flooring option offers versatility with a myriad of color choices available. Different shapes and sizes of tile can be combined to create one-of-a-kind patterns. Current trends with tile include reclaimed wood, faux marble, and metallic finishes.

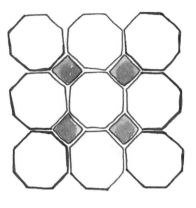

PROS	CONS
• endless design possibilities	• chips easily
• easy to clean	• grout can stain and attract dirt
• affordable	• cold to walk on
• easy to mix and match finishes	• doesn't absorb sound

 TIP

Use tile to make a bold statement in your space. For example, if you want to emphasize your flooring, tile can be your design BFF. Choose oversized or highly pattered tiles and create a graphic design on the floor. You can also change the grout color to add even more visual impact.

Vinyl

Vinyl flooring has come a long way in recent years. The variety of styles and textures is endless, providing flexibility and options with the design. Current trends with vinyl include metallics, faux wood, and faux stone vinyl.

TIP

If you install vinyl flooring, don't throw away the scraps. Reuse and repurpose instead. Line drawers in your home, add vinyl scraps to your garage floor, or even cut sheets for under the sink to protect cabinet surfaces.

PROS	CONS
• extremely affordable	• highly susceptible to nicks and dents
• easy to install	• not durable
• easy to clean	• challenging to repair

Carpet

Carpet is another affordable flooring option that warms up a space and layers in texture and character. Current trends include carpet made from recycled material, cut and loop carpet, and carpet tile.

PROS	CONS
• adds warmth and comfort	• can wear unevenly
• amps up the cozy factor	• stains easily
• comes in a large variety of patterns, colors, and textures	• challenging to clean

● **TIP**

When buying carpet, be sure to ask the retailer if they have any carpet currently in stock. Many times, stores will have excess inventory available at a discount, translating into savings for you.

A Little Inspiration for the Road

● When mixing and matching flooring, start and stop at doorways. This allows each room to have its own personality. Try to keep all types of flooring in the same tone for easy flow.

● If you like the look of hardwood but not the expense or the upkeep, consider installing ceramic tiles that imitate the look of wood. It's a great option with the aesthetic of wood but the easy cleanup of tile.

● Take your flooring to the next level with a mural on the floor. New vinyl flooring products include maps and graphic artwork.

Create patterns with peel and stick tile

Brighten a room with neutrals

Stain a decorative pattern

be the change you hope to see in the world

Add warmth with wood

Questions to Ask Before You Choose Flooring

You've done your research. You've measured and priced and thought and rethought and put one foot in front of the other when it comes to the surfaces on the floors of your rooms. And yet...you're still unsure.

You want to make the right choice. You want to find the best flooring fit. You want to write poems to your flooring too.

Take a moment. Press pause. Then let your fingers do the writing and answer a few questions about your space.

These questions will help you determine which flooring works best for your space. For example, if your style is farmhouse, hardwood flooring might be the perfect fit. If you don't wear shoes in the house, your feet might like carpet. If you are using the space for a craft room, vinyl tile is a great option that can easily be replaced if someone tracks glitter glue all over the floor (not that something like that has ever happened at my house). Your answers to these questions will help you seal the deal (or the grout). Whichever comes first.

Room: _____

What is the purpose of the room?

_____

_____

_____

_____

_____

What is your style?

_____

_____

_____

_____

_____

Who will use it?

_____

_____

_____

_____

_____

_____

How will it be used?

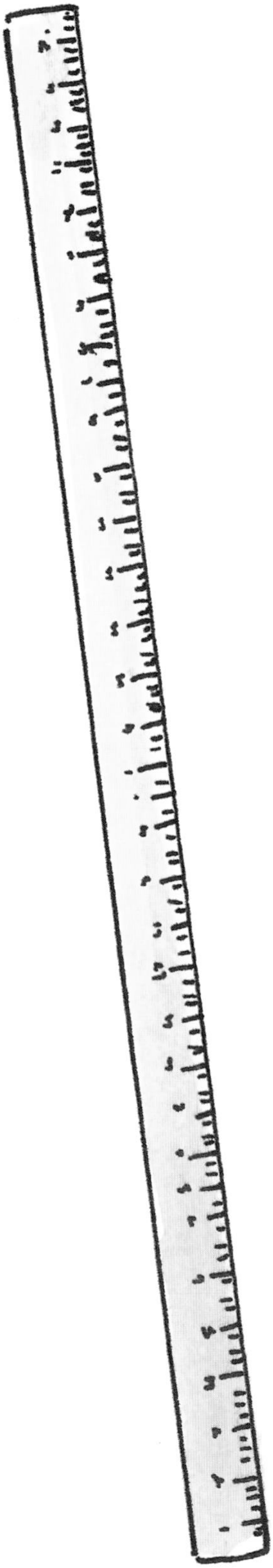

_____

_____

_____

_____

_____

_____

_____

_____

_____

_____

Do you have kids and/or pets?

☐ YES   ☐ NO

Do you wear shoes in the house?

☐ YES   ☐ NO

Are you installing the flooring yourself?

☐ YES   ☐ NO

What is your flooring budget?

$ _____

FLOORING OPTION
Comparison Chart

	Durable?	Easy to Clean?	Absorb Noise?	Cost?	Professional Installation Recommended?	Mood?
Hardwood	✓	✓		$$	✓	Authentic
Laminate	✓	✓		$-$$		Flat
Bamboo	✓	✓		$$-$$$		Modern
Brick	✓		✓	$$$	✓	Character
Tile	✓	✓		$$-$$$	✓	Versatile
Vinyl		✓	✓	$$		Varies
Carpet			✓	$-$$$	✓	Cozy

Wall Treatments

If you are ever on a decorating game show where they hand you fifty dollars and ask you to transform a room in an afternoon—*don't panic*—just ring the buzzer and smile. *You totally got this.* I know it may seem impossible at first glance. Fifty dollars? How can that be? How in the world can anyone transform a room for the cost of a movie night for two with extra popcorn and Junior Mints?

It's actually so much easier than you might think.

All you need is a gallon of paint, some painter's tape, and a little imagination.

Here are some easy and creative ideas for your walls. Each wall treatment lists supplies, skill level, and simple steps to create the look in your own space. You can also add your own notes, ideas, and room measurements for easy reference in the blank pages at the end of this chapter (pages 68 to 69).

DESIGN *life* LESSON

Let your imagination be greater than
the four walls of your room.

☐ paint

☐ paintbrush

☐ painter's tape

☐ level

☐ measuring tape

☐ pencil

 TIP

An odd number of stripes
ensures that the same
colored stripe is on each
corner of the wall (vertical)
or baseboard and ceiling
(horizontal).

Stripes

Stripes are one of the easiest wall treatments to create. Have a small space, such as an entryway or laundry room or mudroom? Stripes are the perfect wall treatment to add a little personality on a budget.

STEPS FOR PAINTING STRIPES

1. Choose the type of stripes you want to add to your space. Horizontal stripes make the room appear wider. Vertical stripes make the room appear taller.

2. Paint your base wall color first. Let dry for 24 hours.

3. Measure off your stripes on the wall with pencil hash marks. Use a level and don't rely on the wall as your guide. Ceilings and walls are not always level, and you don't want to end up with the leaning stripes of Pisa.

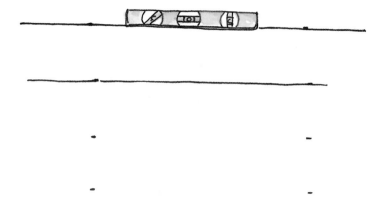

4. A good rule of thumb is to make your stripes between 4" to 12" wide—the smaller your space, the smaller the stripes. If you want to make all your stripes an even size start by measuring the wall. For vertical stripes, measure the width of the wall and then divide the measurement by an odd number. For horizontal stripes, measure the height of the wall instead and divide the measurement by an odd number as well.

5. Tape off the *outside* of the stripe with painter's tape. Mark the stripe to be painted with a small piece of tape to help you paint the correct one. Do NOT skip this step. Take it from a professional stripe painter. It's so easy to mis-paint.

TIP

You can also create a subtle stripe wall treatment with different finishes of the same color of paint. For example, you could paint shiny stripes with matte stripes in the same color.

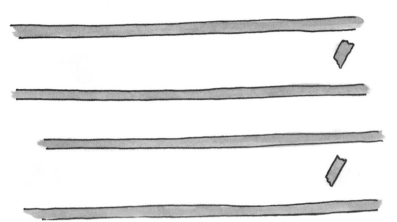

6. Carefully pull off the tape while the paint is still wet to prevent paint from seeping under the tape and drying. This will ensure the paint lines are perfect.

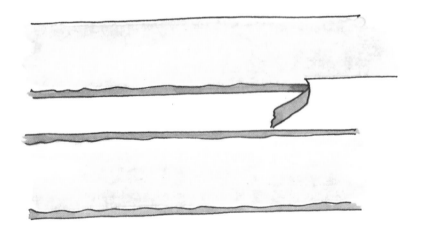

Faux Molding

SUPPLIES

☐ paint

☐ paintbrush

☐ painter's tape

☐ level

☐ measuring tape

☐ pencil

Sometimes installing molding can be overwhelming. But here's the thing. Molding has a cousin that's inexpensive and less permanent and can be added to a room in an afternoon. Meet your new friend...faux molding.

One of the easiest faux molding treatments is faux panels. Instead of actual three-dimensional molding, create the same look with paint.

STEPS FOR PAINTING FAUX PANELS

1. Start with a blank accent wall and tape off a row of oversized vertical rectangles with painter's tape.

2. Next, tape two more rows of painter's tape directly outside the original rectangle. When you're finished, you should have three rectangles taped—one slightly larger than the next.

3. Remove the center strip of tape. This gives you a perfectly spaced frame to paint.

4. Paint the entire rectangle frame and remove the tape when the paint is wet. Repeat for the rest of the faux panels on the wall.

● TIP

Some other ideas include faux molding over the top of windows and doors, faux chair rail panels, and faux picture frame molding.

Ombre Wall

SKILL LEVEL

Intermediate

SUPPLIES

☐ paint

☐ paintbrush

☐ painter's tape

☐ level

☐ measuring tape

☐ pencil

Ombre is so current. So now. It's so hip and cool and major and trendy and cutting edge that your wall will be the talk of the house (and the neighborhood).

STEPS FOR PAINTING AN OMBRE WALL

1. Begin by choosing your color palette. Find a paint chip in a particular hue that you like. Buy every paint color on the paint strip.

2. Mark off the entire wall with horizontal stripes approximately 16" apart. If you have 8' ceilings, that measurement translates to 6 horizontal stripes on the wall. You may need to adjust the width of the stripes depending on the height of your ceilings. *(Be sure and follow the directions under the stripe section.)*

3. Tape off every other stripe on the *outside* of your marks with painter's tape.

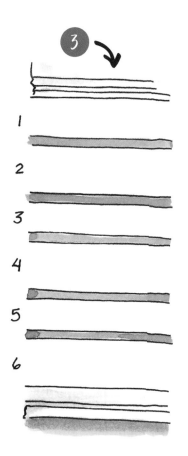

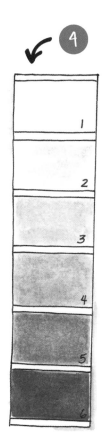

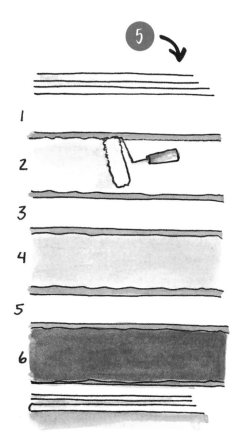

4. Number your colors on the paint strip from 1 to 6, 1 as the lightest and 6 as the darkest.

5. Starting at the bottom of the wall, paint the darkest color on the paint strip (number 6). Then, paint the next taped stripe with the color marked number 4. Paint the next taped stripe with the color marked number 2. Remove the tape and let the paint dry for 24 hours.

6. Tape off the remaining horizontal stripes on the *outside* so that you can paint the remaining stripes.

7. Starting with the second stripe from the bottom, paint it with the color marked number 5. Then paint the next taped stripe with the color marked number 3. Paint the next taped stripe next to the ceiling with the color marked number 1.

8. Remove the painter's tape immediately.

TIP

There are many different variations on the ombre wall. You could add the ombre treatment to three quarters or even half of the wall, or continue the ombre color pattern onto the floor. You could also ombre the wall colors vertically instead of horizontally.

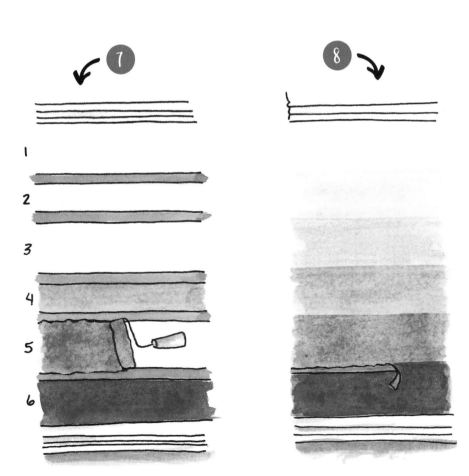

Checks

This paint treatment is a fun way to add a little whimsy to a game room or craft room. It's kind of like painting stripes, but it goes all fancy and takes it to the next level.

STEPS FOR PAINTING CHECKS

1. Choose two contrasting colors for your checks. Start by painting your wall the base color. Let dry for 24 hours.

2. Mark off the entire wall with horizontal stripes approximately 12" apart. Tape off the *outside* of the stripe with painter's tape. You can make your stripes wider if you want to paint larger checks (*be sure and follow the directions under the stripe section*).

3. Paint the selected stripes with the color you've selected for the other check. Remove tape and let dry for 24 hours.

4. Tape off the entire wall with vertical stripes approximately 12" apart. Remember to tape the *outside* of the stripes you will be painting. If you made your horizontal stripes wider, then you will need to make your vertical stripes wider to match.

5. Paint every other vertical stripe with the same color you used to paint the horizontal stripes. Remove tape and let dry for 24 hours.

SKILL LEVEL

Intermediate

SUPPLIES

- [ ] paint
- [ ] paintbrush
- [ ] painter's tape
- [ ] level
- [ ] measuring tape
- [ ] pencil

 TIP

You can take your check wall treatment to the next level and tape off thin vertical and horizontal stripes in contrasting colors to create a plaid.

Faux Brick

SKILL LEVEL

Advanced

SUPPLIES

☐ paint

☐ paintbrush

☐ thin painter's tape

☐ level

☐ measuring tape

☐ pencil

☐ sea sponge

 TIP

This wall treatment idea is perfect in a transitional room, such as a hallway or entryway. It draws attention to a room that's overlooked. A faux brick wall helps to give a small space a big personality.

Create an accent wall in a space with a faux brick wall. This treatment is easier to add to a space than traditional brick pavers, a lot less expensive, and the mortar always stays clean.

STEPS FOR PAINTING BRICK

1. Start by painting your accent wall the color you want your mortar to be. Let dry for 24 hours.

2. Mark off the wall with horizontal stripes approximately 5" apart (*be sure and follow the directions under the stripe section*). You can make your stripes wider if you want to paint larger bricks.

3. Tape off the entire wall with horizontal stripes. Use ⅛" painter's tape for this project to create a more realistic-looking wall.

4. After the horizontal stripes are taped off, go back and place a vertical piece of painter's tape every 9" between the two pieces of horizontal tape (or wider if you altered your brick size in step 2). Stagger the vertical pieces of tape to mimic bricks.

5. Paint the accent wall with a brick color. Let dry 24 hours.

6. To add additional depth to your bricks, you can dip a sea sponge in a mixture of one-third water to two-thirds burnt umber glaze. Then lightly sponge a layer of the glaze/water mixture on top of the painted bricks.

7. Remove the tape to show the mortar underneath.

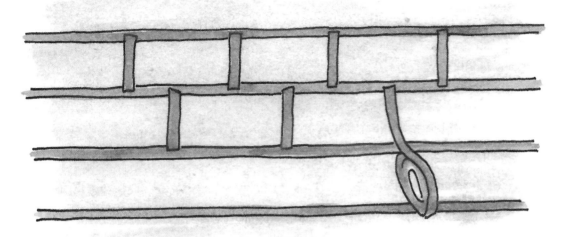

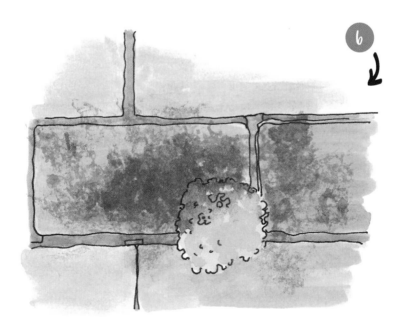

TEMPORARY WALL
Treatment Ideas

Sometimes a wall can't be painted. For a variety of reasons, whether you're a renter or about to move, or paint seems like a giant commitment, sometimes a room needs a temporary wall treatment instead. If you are looking for something that's not truly permanent, this section is for you.

STENCILED DROP CLOTHS—Stencil drop cloths from the hardware store with fabric paint. Hang the drop cloths on an accent wall with dowel rods cut to fit the space and hung on brackets (similar to curtains) for an additional layer of texture.

TEMPORARY WALLPAPER—This product is just like a contact paper for walls and comes in a variety of patterns and colors. Follow manufacturer's instructions to ensure easy removal.

FOAM BOARD COVERS—Purchase 20" x 30" foam boards and cover the boards with fabric. Attach the boards to the wall with removable adhesive strips for a pop of color that can be easily taken down.

RECIPE WALL—Add your favorite recipe to an accent wall with vinyl letters and numbers. Tape off vertical lines as a guide to make sure your recipe is straight.

VINYL WALL DECALS—Vinyl decals come in a variety of shapes, including polka dots, stripes, Bible verses, and quotes. Decorate a wall in minutes with this easy-to-apply product.

Plan Your Wall Treatment Project

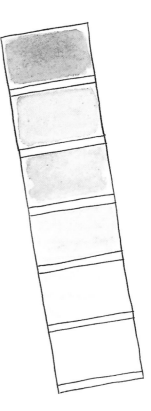

1. Look at your overall design plan and select a room where a wall treatment might work.

2. Visualize it in your space to make sure it fits your design aesthetic.

3. Take measurements and sketch out the dimensions of your blank wall on graph paper provided on page 68. Make sure to take doors, windows, and other architectural features into account.

4. Do your math.

5. Sketch your wall treatment design to scale.

6. Choose your colors and purchase paint.

7. Follow project steps.

8. Step back, look at the finished project, and tell yourself how amazing you are.

A Little Inspiration for the Road

- Stencils are another great option for an accent wall. You can purchase oversized room stencils online in a variety of design styles.

- Make sure you have all the tools necessary for the project before you get started. Nothing cramps inspiration's style more than four trips to the home improvement store.

- Find the wall treatment project you like and embrace it. Put your own spin on a classic. One of my twin daughters covered an entire wall with Bible verses and inspirational quotes written on different color Post-it Notes. She loves her wall, and I would never change it. It's perfect for her. There's only one you, and what you love will work in your home.

Paint
contrasting
stripes

Design
a piece
of art

3/4 CUP SUGAR

2 EGGS

1 CUP CRANBERRIES

Create
a recipe
wall

Try
vertical
stripes
to add
drama

SKETCH YOUR WALL TREATMENT PROJECT

W indow treatments are a lot like jewelry. I'm a vintage rhinestone necklace with layers of sparkle and amethyst beads.

How about you?

And just as a colorful pair of statement earrings or a set of shiny bangle bracelets create the perfect accent pieces for an outfit, curtains and shades and shutters and panels do the same for a room. Some of us like our window treatments big and bold and over the top. Some of us like simple and classic and clean design options for our windows.

The key is selecting the right window jewelry for each of our rooms. Here are a few basic guidelines to select the perfect options for your space.

DESIGN *life* LESSON

Windows frame the view to the
world outside. Let the sunshine in.

HELPFUL
Window Treatment Terms

When choosing options for your window coverings, it's a good idea to research all your options. After all, there's more to a window than simple drapery panels. Here are a few window treatment terms to get you started.

BLINDS
A window covering with slats that open and close to let in light. Blinds can also be adjusted vertically.

CORNICE
A curtain header typically constructed of wood placed over the top part of a window. Many times, it's used in place of a fabric valance.

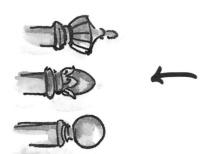

FINIALS
The decorative piece fastened to the end of a curtain rod.

HAND
The actual feel and draping of the fabric used to create the window treatment.

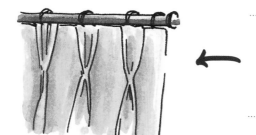

PINCH PLEATS
Folded formal pleats used at the top of a drapery panel.

PLEATED HEADING
A type of curtain constructed as a stationary panel with permanent pleating. This is used in conjunction with a traverse rod.

ROD POCKET HEADING

A type of curtain constructed with a sewn pocket for the curtain rod.

ROLLER SHADE

A window shade mounted on a roller that retracts when pulled up.

ROMAN SHADES

A type of shade where the fabric is stacked up in the window rather than rolled up like a roller shade.

SHEERS

Lightweight, thin panels that allow light in. These are used for privacy.

SHUTTERS

A window treatment with moveable louvered folding pieces designed to cover the window completely when closed. Shutters are built into a frame designed to fit inside (or just outside) the window.

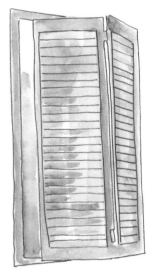

SWING ARM ROD

A type of curtain rod attached to the wall or window frame that swings out away from the window and functions like a shutter.

TAB TOP HEADING

A type of curtain with tabs sewed onto the top of the curtain. The curtain can be gathered on one end or pulled across the rod.

Add a Little Width

You don't want wimpy curtains. Extra width is your friend. Make sure your curtains are full, with lots of volume and a little extra fluff. A good rule of thumb for width measurement is to make sure your curtain width is two to two and a half times the width of the window. If you intend for your curtains to remain stationary, each panel should measure one and a half times the width of your window.

 TIP

Another insider window treatment tip? Hang the curtain rods 5" or 6" outside the window frame to create the illusion the windows are larger than they actually are.

TIP

Not all curtains need tiebacks. Pleated curtains or hooked curtains typically hang straight down. But when tiebacks are needed, why not think outside the box? Create a tieback from a bracelet or gold link chain. Or use a ribbon, jute twine with an industrial clasp, or a colorful scarf to hold the curtains in place.

Consider the Curtain Length

To puddle or not to puddle? Curtain length is extremely important.

Too-short curtains with high-waters are a definite no-no.

Instead, opt for a more tailored look with panels that extend to no more than a ½" above the floor. This length is perfect for window treatments that are opened and closed often.

Looking for a more forgiving curtain length option? Create a mini fabric puddle with an additional 1" to 2" of hem length. This length is ideal for an older home with uneven floors or varying window heights.

Lastly, for a high-end look with a little more maintenance, add an additional 3" to 4" of fabric to the hem to create a glamourous puddle-look for your curtain panels.

DETERMINE YOUR CURTAIN
Length & Width

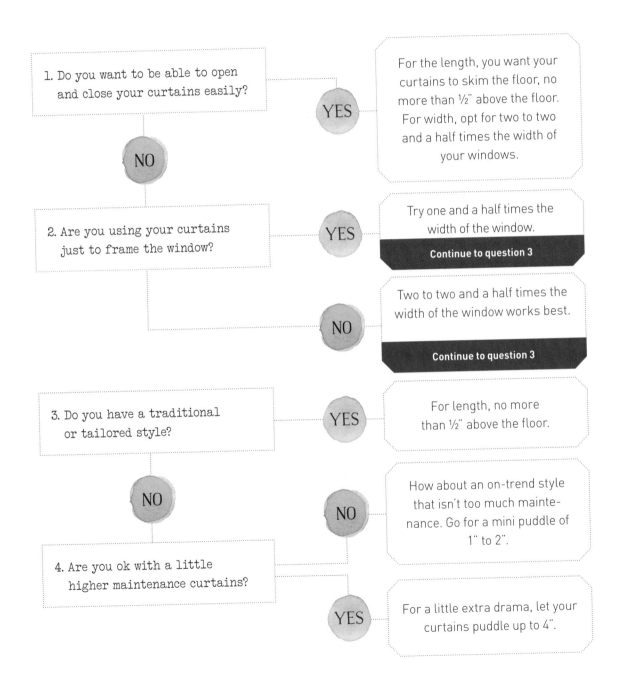

1. Do you want to be able to open and close your curtains easily?

YES — For the length, you want your curtains to skim the floor, no more than ½" above the floor. For width, opt for two to two and a half times the width of your windows.

NO

2. Are you using your curtains just to frame the window?

YES — Try one and a half times the width of the window.

Continue to question 3

NO — Two to two and a half times the width of the window works best.

Continue to question 3

3. Do you have a traditional or tailored style?

YES — For length, no more than ½" above the floor.

NO — How about an on-trend style that isn't too much maintenance. Go for a mini puddle of 1" to 2".

NO

4. Are you ok with a little higher maintenance curtains?

YES — For a little extra drama, let your curtains puddle up to 4".

Select Fabric

One important factor when choosing your window treatments is to select the right fabric for the room. The same style of curtains in an alternative fabric can create an entirely different look in a space. Here are some rooms and the fabrics that love them:

KITCHEN
Lightweight cotton; many times, kitchen curtains are unlined to let light in.

DINING ROOM
Dramatic fabrics, such as velvet or linen or silk, work well in this room.

LIVING ROOM
Linen or cotton works well in this space; fabrics are typically lined for a more formal look.

BEDROOM
Casual fabrics, such as polished cotton or lightweight cotton, work well in this space. If privacy is an issue, blackout curtains are also an option.

PORCH
For an outdoor room or a space open to the elements, indoor/outdoor fabrics are the best choice.

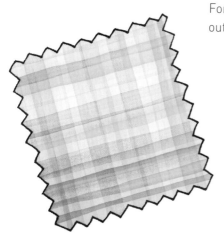

CHOOSE YOUR
Fabric Type

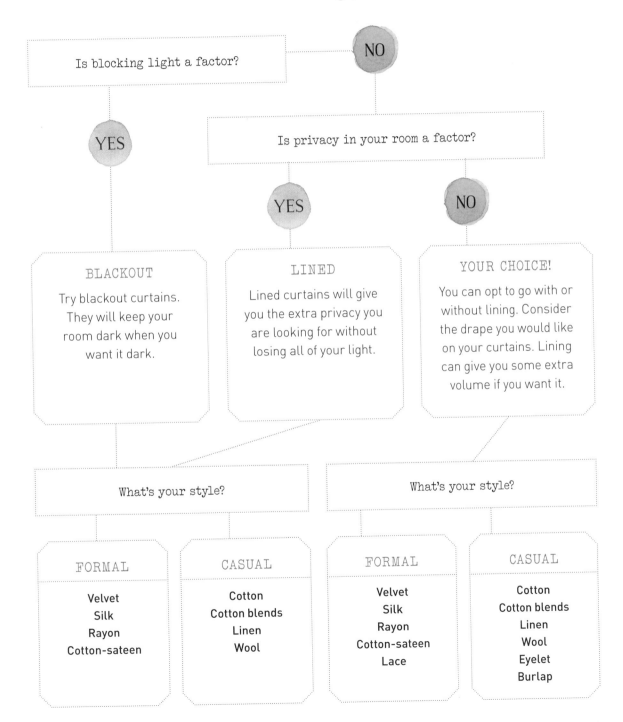

Is blocking light a factor?

NO

YES

Is privacy in your room a factor?

YES

NO

BLACKOUT

Try blackout curtains. They will keep your room dark when you want it dark.

LINED

Lined curtains will give you the extra privacy you are looking for without losing all of your light.

YOUR CHOICE!

You can opt to go with or without lining. Consider the drape you would like on your curtains. Lining can give you some extra volume if you want it.

What's your style?

What's your style?

FORMAL

Velvet
Silk
Rayon
Cotton-sateen

CASUAL

Cotton
Cotton blends
Linen
Wool

FORMAL

Velvet
Silk
Rayon
Cotton-sateen
Lace

CASUAL

Cotton
Cotton blends
Linen
Wool
Eyelet
Burlap

Dream About Color and Pattern Options

Color and pattern are the heart of any window treatment selection. Curtains are typically the largest textile surface in a space and a great place to showcase your personality. Leaning toward a bold, graphic design? Select a large-scale overall pattern. Trending toward neutral? Select a fabric with a small-scale design or a fabric with a slight texture. Choosing a monochromatic look for your space? Perhaps consider curtains the same color as your wall. This creates a classic, neutral backdrop for the rest of the design for your space.

 NOTE

Roman shades are a classic, affordable option for window treatments. They can be relaxed, more formal, or even fixed in place.

 TIP

Install roman shades by themselves or combine the shades with longer curtain panels to elongate the height of the window. To create this look, simply install a standard curtain rod 6" to 7" above the window frame. Next, install roman shades 6" to 7" above the frame behind the curtain rods.

PICK YOUR
Pattern & Color

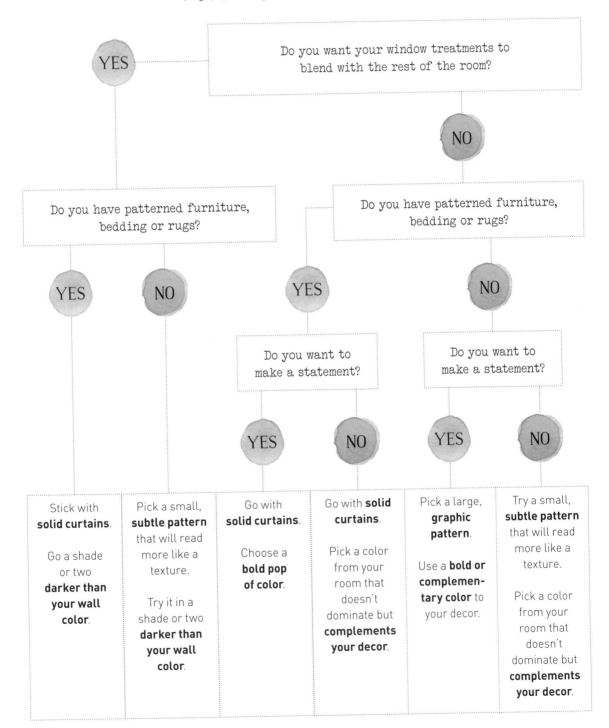

Do you want your window treatments to blend with the rest of the room?

YES

NO

Do you have patterned furniture, bedding or rugs?

Do you have patterned furniture, bedding or rugs?

YES

NO

YES

NO

Do you want to make a statement?

Do you want to make a statement?

YES

NO

YES

NO

Stick with **solid curtains**.

Go a shade or two **darker than your wall color**.

Pick a small, **subtle pattern** that will read more like a texture.

Try it in a shade or two **darker than your wall color**.

Go with **solid curtains**.

Choose a **bold pop of color**.

Go with **solid curtains**.

Pick a color from your room that doesn't dominate but **complements your decor**.

Pick a large, **graphic pattern**.

Use a **bold or complementary color** to your decor.

Try a small, **subtle pattern** that will read more like a texture.

Pick a color from your room that doesn't dominate but **complements your decor**.

Choose Your Curtain Rod Wisely

All curtain rods are not created equal. There are four basic types of curtain rods, each rod is used for different purposes and different types of curtains.

BASIC CURTAIN ROD

This rod attaches to the wall with brackets, and this versatile rod can be used with most types of panels, including tab top and rod pocket curtains.

RETURN ROD

This rod is often used to wrap the curtains around the rounded end of the rod and extend the edge of the panel to the wall. Return rods are a good option for reducing light in a space.

CAFÉ CURTAINS ↗

TENSION ROD

This rod is often used to hang café curtains inside the window frame. It is a great option for showcasing the window's molding.

TRAVERSE ROD

This rod is used with pleated or hooked curtains that are stationary and pulled across the length of the rod. This rod works well with curtains that are opened and closed often.

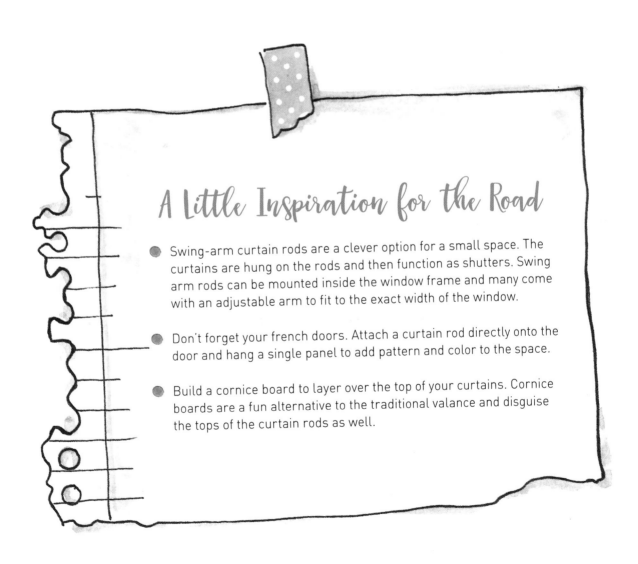

A Little Inspiration for the Road

- Swing-arm curtain rods are a clever option for a small space. The curtains are hung on the rods and then function as shutters. Swing arm rods can be mounted inside the window frame and many come with an adjustable arm to fit to the exact width of the window.

- Don't forget your french doors. Attach a curtain rod directly onto the door and hang a single panel to add pattern and color to the space.

- Build a cornice board to layer over the top of your curtains. Cornice boards are a fun alternative to the traditional valance and disguise the tops of the curtain rods as well.

Make curtains from drop cloths

Create a valence with vintage pennants

Add texture with smocking

Hang rods
above window
frame for
a dramatic
effect

Let's talk about lighting—otherwise known as a design speed bump. Choosing lighting is often the part of the decorating process where so many of us become stuck. We walk into a lighting store and stare up at the chandeliers and pendant lights and wall sconces as the fixtures stare back at us, glittering and shimmering—looking all beautiful and glamourous and above our pay grade. How is a person supposed to choose? How can you know which lighting fixture will look best? How can you determine what chandelier goes in what room? There are a lot of choices, and they can all be a little overwhelming.

Can I get an amen?

No worries. You've tackled space planning, paint colors, flooring options, and wall and window treatments. This whole lighting thing should be a walk in the park—especially with a little help. Good thing I've tackled many design lighting speed bumps along the way and discovered a few things *not* to do. Here are some tips to help make all your lighting dreams come true.

DESIGN *Life* LESSON

Lighting has a way of illuminating and reminding us what's truly important in life.

Choose the Right-Sized Fixture

Nothing can overwhelm or underwhelm a room more than a fixture that's wrong for a space. Show that light fixture who's boss. Here are a few basic measurement guidelines broken down by room.

OPEN AREAS

Here's an easy way to determine the size of the light fixture you need for a large open space, such as a living room.

$$\frac{\text{Length of the room (in feet)} + \text{Width of the room (in feet)}}{\text{Light fixture diameter or width (in inches)}}$$

For example:

12' + 12' = 24" light fixture

 TIP

Allow 7' of clearance under any fixture in an open space.

HALLWAYS

You want to make sure a hallway is well lit to avoid dark corners. Typically, a light fixture is needed every 8 feet. When determining the number of lights you'll need for a hallway...

$$\frac{\text{Length of the hallway (feet)}}{8} = \text{number of lights}$$

For example:

$$\frac{16'}{8'} = 2 \text{ light fixtures}$$

DINING ROOM

For the right-sized light fixture in your dining room...

$$\frac{\text{Length of the table (in inches)}}{\text{Maximum chandelier width (in inches)}} - 12$$

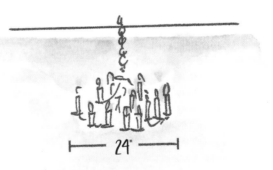

For example:

36" − 12 = 24" chandelier

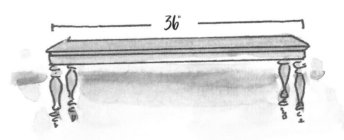

Hang Lights at the Correct Height

This is one of the most common mistakes made in lighting. You want to make sure your lighting is hung in a way that's pleasing to the eye. Want specifics? Here are a few good measurements to follow:

WALL FIXTURES

Sconces and wall fixtures should be hung on the wall at least 74" from the floor. Remember to take your ceiling height into account as well to ensure the fixtures are not too close to the ceiling.

DOORWAYS

Hang entryway lighting at least 6" taller than the door.

BATHROOMS
The lighting fixture selected for above the mirror should be at least one-third its width. When selecting two fixtures for the vanity area, place them at least 28" apart to prevent shadows in the mirror. When installing a sconce on either side of a mirror, a good rule of thumb is to leave approximately 4 to 5 inches of space between the sconce and the edge of the mirror.

Layer Lighting

When designing the lighting for a space, ensure the room has layers of lighting for different tasks. Layering in different sources of light transforms the overall feel of a room with the flip of a switch. A good rule of thumb is to layer in at least three different points of light in a space. For example, a living room might have a table lamp, a floor lamp, and recessed lighting or a chandelier. A kitchen may have a pendant light over the sink, a table lamp on a counter, and a light fixture over the kitchen table.

● TIP

Have you noticed a trend with design in threes? Just remember that when in doubt, stick with an odd number.

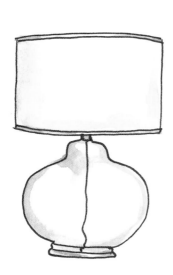

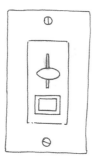

Install Dimmer Switches

Not all lighting tasks are created equal. Sometimes a task requires a lot of light, and sometimes the task calls for a warm subtle glow to a space. One of the most inexpensive (and often overlooked) ways to change up your lighting is with a dimmer switch. Most dimmer switches are easy to install, save energy, and extend the life of lightbulbs.

Consider the Bulb Color

Have you ever walked into a room and something felt a little off? The room felt too cool, or there was an odd yellow cast to the walls? Chances are it was the bulb's fault. Choosing the correct bulb can make all the difference in the light and feel of a space. Either a warm light or a clear, bright light is the best option for most spaces.

Unless you are having a '70s party, and then you'll want to install disco lights. Obvi.

● TIP

Be kind to the planet. Select energy-efficient bulbs for the fixtures in your space.

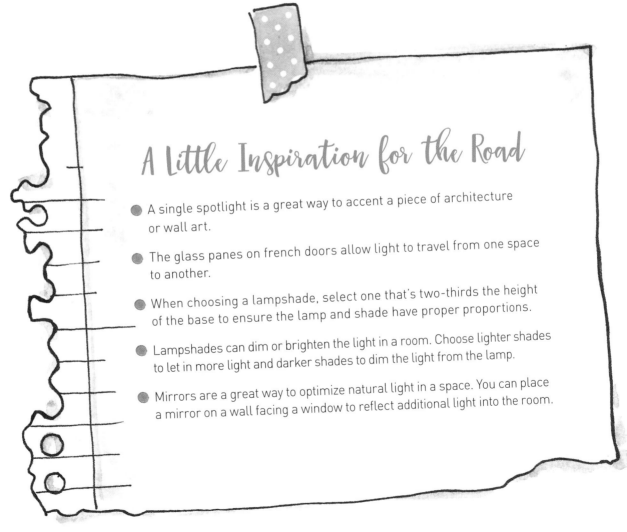

A Little Inspiration for the Road

- A single spotlight is a great way to accent a piece of architecture or wall art.

- The glass panes on french doors allow light to travel from one space to another.

- When choosing a lampshade, select one that's two-thirds the height of the base to ensure the lamp and shade have proper proportions.

- Lampshades can dim or brighten the light in a room. Choose lighter shades to let in more light and darker shades to dim the light from the lamp.

- Mirrors are a great way to optimize natural light in a space. You can place a mirror on a wall facing a window to reflect additional light into the room.

FIND YOUR
LIGHTING
STYLE

TABLE   FLOOR

TRADITIONAL

FARMHOUSE

MODERN

SCONCE　　　　PENDANT　　　　CHANDELIER

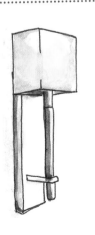

Try a patterned shade

Go classic with a drum shade

Add texture with a beaded chandelier

Add different types of task lighting

Pattern Mixing

Mixing textiles and patterns is a lot like the recipe on the back of the chocolate chips package. If you follow the directions and add the right amount of flour and sugar and butter and eggs, the cookies turn out perfectly every time. This same principle applies to mixing patterns. Have you ever selected fabric for a room and something wasn't right? You knew something was off, but you couldn't figure out what to adjust.

Just look to the cookie for inspiration. The answer is in the recipe.

One of the easiest ways to change the look and feel of a room is to layer different patterns with your textiles. The key is knowing what to mix with what—especially with pillows and throws and curtains and cushions. Once you learn the guidelines, you'll understand where things go and if you've added too much vanilla to the recipe. Here are a few simple tried-and-true methods for figuring out what patterns work in your space.

DESIGN *life* LESSON

Pattern your life like your textiles. Always remember to add in the fun.

Embrace the Rule
of Odd Numbers

Your pattern doesn't need to be odd, but the number of patterns you choose should be. Have you ever noticed how things look better when grouped in odd numbers? Three candlesticks on the mantel. Five frames on the wall. Seven vases in a centerpiece. That same rule applies here.

When selecting your patterns for a room, stick with odd numbers.

Start with three patterns and add more if needed.

 NOTE

Mix and match your own pattern combinations. See pages 108–109.

Scale It Up

When mixing patterns, it's important to keep scale in mind. Begin with the largest-scale pattern first and use this as your guide. Make sure this is a pattern you love and build your room around it. This large-scale pattern sets the tone for the entire space.

Then select a second pattern that's half the scale of the first pattern. This fabric doesn't need to mimic the design of the first fabric you've chosen—the key is in adjusting the scale. For example, if you have a large overall floral, layer it with a medium buffalo check.

Next, round out the pattern rodeo with an even smaller design. Here's where you can add in tiny stripes or little polka dots or miniature seahorses blowing bubbles. Choose this pattern wisely. You don't want it to be so small that it translates as a solid and disappears when viewed from a distance. No one likes an invisible sea horse.

SMALL SCALE

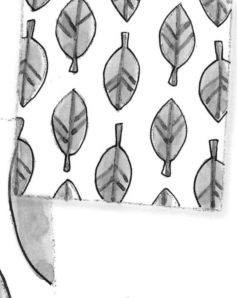

MEDIUM SCALE

LARGE SCALE

Create a Color Palette

Creating a palette is easy if you start and end with the color wheel. Here are a few important things to note about this helpful tool. Find a color you like and then trace your finger across the wheel to the color on the opposite side. This is your color's BFF. It's known as its complementary color. Orange, meet Blue. Red, meet Green. Purple, meet Yellow, and so on.

To find a good contrasting color, simply look to another segment of the color wheel. Here's a good rule of thumb when looking for contrasting colors—the more colors between the two choices on the color wheel, the more contrast. For example, there is much more contrast between red and yellow than red and orange, which are closer together on the wheel. Using contrasting or complementary colors will create a vibrant look for your room.

Look at your color again, now check out your color's neighbors. Do you love cool colors like blues, greens, and purples or warm colors like yellow, oranges, and reds? These neighbors are known as analogous colors. Analogous colors work well together can be used together to create a palette with a serene or comforting design.

STEPS TO CREATE A COLOR PALETTE

1. Start with a color you love.

2. Are you more drawn to its neighbors or contrasting color?

3. From there, determine your dominant color, secondary color, and an accent color. (Don't forget the power of a good neutral!)

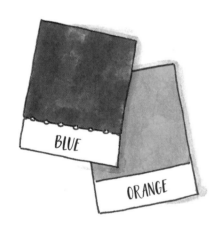

Add Pattern to Your Palette

When mixing patterns, one of the easiest ways to make your patterns blend is to stick with the same color intensity when making fabric choices. For example, if you start with bright, happy, vibrant colors, choose that same color palette for all the patterns in a space. If you choose neutral, less vibrant colors, stick with muted tones with the rest of the color choices in your patterns. Selecting similar hues ensures your room feels finished and well planned.

Color Wheel

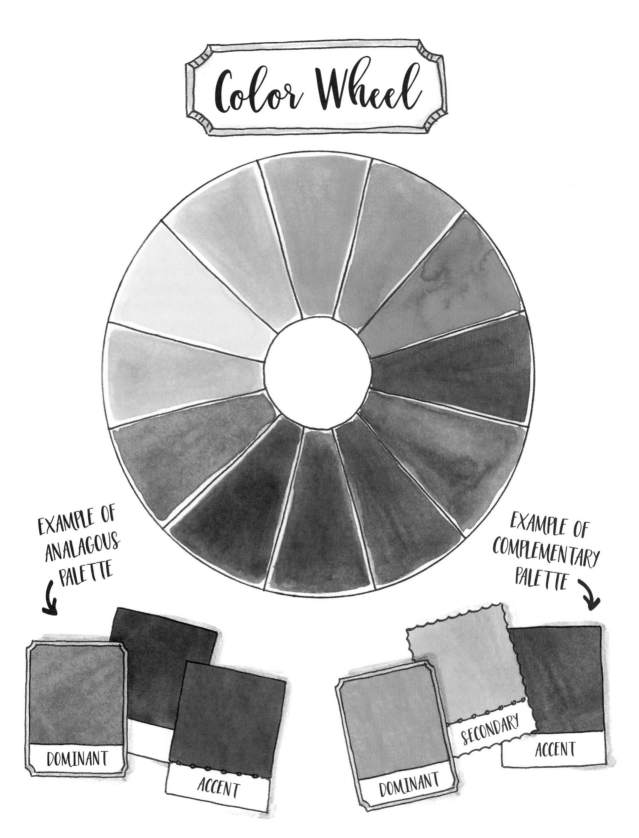

EXAMPLE OF ANALAGOUS PALETTE

DOMINANT

ACCENT

EXAMPLE OF COMPLEMENTARY PALETTE

SECONDARY

ACCENT

DOMINANT

Follow the Formula

To decide how much of each pattern to add to a space,

simply follow the 60/30/10 rule.

Select the pattern you like the best, and use it in 60 percent of your design choices. Add a smaller coordinating pattern for 30 percent of the design choices, and use the remaining pattern 10 percent of the time. This is just a guideline to follow and can easily be adjusted if you choose more than three patterns for a space.

Using this principle, it's easy to change the look of a space just by changing which pattern is emphasized. For example, if you use your large-scale pattern 60 percent of the time, the room will have more of an emphasis on textiles. If you use a medium-scale pattern 60 percent of the time, the fabric may stand out less in a space.

Repeat and Balance Patterns

It's important to remember that all the fabrics you choose don't have to be different designs. For example, you can easily choose two florals for a room. Or two polka dots. Or two geometric patterns. Just vary the size and scale of the design with each choice. This gives each pattern a voice and an individual seat at the table.

When designing your space, make sure not to glump all the patterns together on one side of the room. Glumping patterns (a totally official design term) makes a room feel lopsided. Too much togetherness works against your design choices. Make sure you spread out your pattern across the room to create a space that's cohesive.

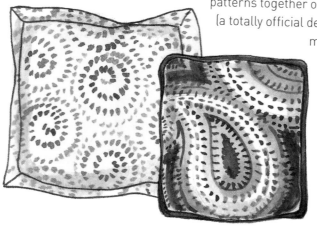

Think Solid

When mixing patterns, it easy to forget about a solid. When chasing curls and swirls and stripes and swishes, the solid often doesn't get invited to the party.

Never underestimate the function of an amazing solid-colored fabric.

A solid is called a solid for a reason. It lives up to its name. A simple, solid pattern lets the eye rest. It lets the room breath. It provides a break from all those dots and stripes and ivy vines.

TIP

Solids don't have to be boring. If you are looking to add texture to a space, a solid is a great place to start. Add a woven fabric or a velvet or a linen to give your fabric a little personality.

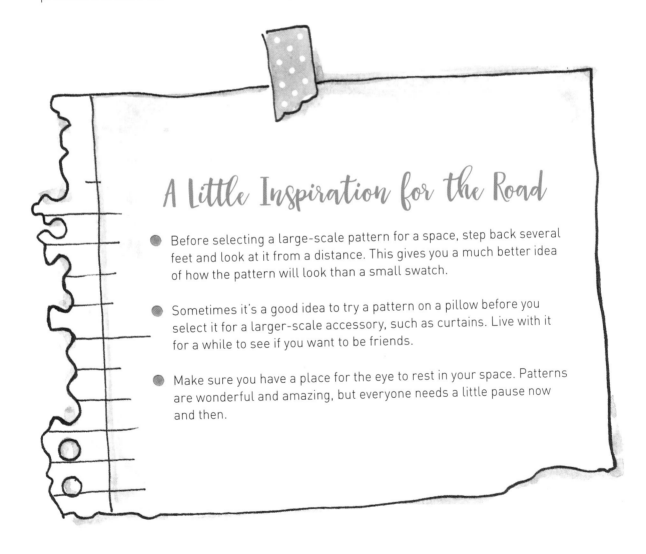

A Little Inspiration for the Road

- Before selecting a large-scale pattern for a space, step back several feet and look at it from a distance. This gives you a much better idea of how the pattern will look than a small swatch.

- Sometimes it's a good idea to try a pattern on a pillow before you select it for a larger-scale accessory, such as curtains. Live with it for a while to see if you want to be friends.

- Make sure you have a place for the eye to rest in your space. Patterns are wonderful and amazing, but everyone needs a little pause now and then.

Combine color and texture

Mix stripes and florals

Choose different scale patterns

Remember the 60/30/10 rule

PATTERN MIXING
By Style

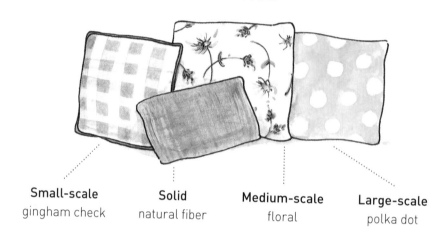

Small-scale
gingham check

Solid
natural fiber

Medium-scale
floral

Large-scale
polka dot

NEUTRAL

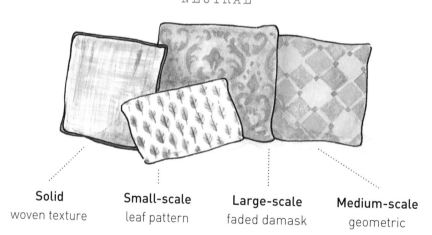

Solid
woven texture

Small-scale
leaf pattern

Large-scale
faded damask

Medium-scale
geometric

BOLD

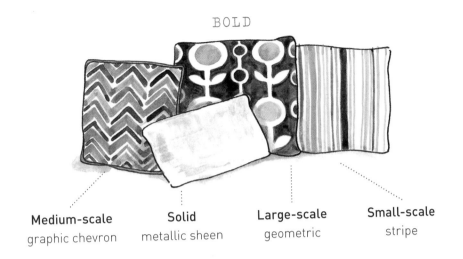

Medium-scale
graphic chevron

Solid
metallic sheen

Large-scale
geometric

Small-scale
stripe

TRADITIONAL

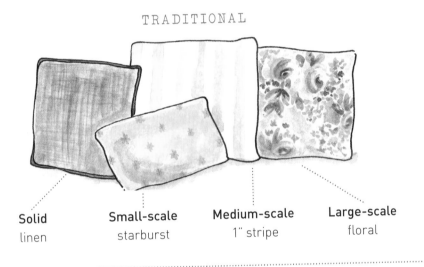

Solid
linen

Small-scale
starburst

Medium-scale
1" stripe

Large-scale
floral

WHIMSICAL

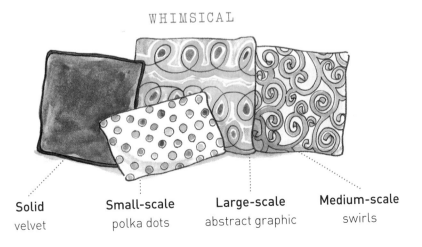

Solid
velvet

Small-scale
polka dots

Large-scale
abstract graphic

Medium-scale
swirls

CREATE YOUR OWN
PATTERN COMBOS AND
PASTE THEM HERE.

USE FABRIC
SWATCHES OR PILLOWS
ON PAGE 133

Accessory Styling

Don't tell the other chapters, but this one is my favorite. It needs its own theme song with extra drum rolls and a trumpet solo because there's nothing an accessory can't do. It can leap bookcases in a single bound. It can save a hutch that's about to make a wrong turn. It can rescue a wall that's lost its way and a kitchen island that's far from home.

An accessory puts the coffee in table.

You can find accessories anywhere. Pick them up at yard sales and thrift stores and your grandmother's attic. You can make your own accessories for spaces in your home in an afternoon. You can tweak them and twist them and turn them this way and that and make sure they have friends.

This is where design becomes fun.

This is the place to showcase your personality and your heart and that one-of-a-kind overstuffed ottoman with swimming mermaids you found at an auction. This is your house and your space, and you want to decorate it with things you love. If you are looking for a few ideas for some creative and unique accessories for your home, you have come to the right chapter.

Here are some of my favorite think-outside-the-box-you'll-never-believe-what-I-did-with-that-who-knew-a-yard-sale-find-could-look-so-good ideas.

DESIGN *life* LESSON

Accessories are a girl's (and a home's) best friend.

YARD SALE
Watch List

Make sure to keep an eye out for these popular collector's items at yard sales.

ARCHITECTURAL REMNANTS—These make great wall art.

BASKETS—If you don't like the color, spray paint is your friend.

MASON JARS—These are the best inexpensive vases ever.

SHUTTERS—Use them for height or texture in your display.

STATE PLATES—Collect plates from different parts of the country.

STOOLS—These kind of count as furniture, but they needed their own byline.

VINTAGE FRAMES—The chippier the better.

VINTAGE SILVER PLATE PIECES—Mix and match your patterns.

WHITEWARE—You can never have enough white dishes and a few of their relatives.

WOODEN FURNITURE—Look at the lines of a piece, not the color.

Stack Your Way to a Stylish Coffee Table

Looking for a signature
piece for your space? Why
not personalize your coffee
table with paint? Using a
stencil, create a pattern
on the top of the table in
a complimentary color to
existing paint color on the
table top. Let dry, seal
with a water based sealer,
and then finish off your
transformed table with a
vase full of fresh flowers.

When styling a coffee table, you want to start with something
low—a basket, tray, or platter. Next, stack books or group objects
that are different heights.

The key is to vary your coffee table display
silhouette.

Lastly, add some texture to the display. Greenery or branches
or wood beads all add a layer of texture to the grouping. Here are
some ideas for unique accessories.

RE-COVER SOME OLD BOOKS

Using scrapbook paper that matches your decor, cover the books (remember fourth grade—go all old school). Cut out a rectangle slightly larger than the book and fold to make a cover. Write the name of the book on the spine or print out title labels and display your books in style. Then stack the books in groups of three and add a mason jar filled with flowersto the display.

FIND A BASKET AND STENCIL IT

Select a low, flat basket and then, using basic stencils and craft paint, add your name and the year your house was built. Place in the center of the coffee table and fill it with books and magazines.

STITCH A WOODEN TRAY

Take a simple wood tray from a thrift store and stitch it. Print out the word you want to stitch on the computer and trace onto the bottom left-hand of the tray using carbon paper. Then mark each of the traced letters with tiny dots about 1" apart. Drill holes in each of the dots and stitch up each of the letters with embroidery thread. Place the tray in the center of the coffee table, and fill it up with different sizes of grapevine spheres.

Add Space for a Novel Bookcase

TIP

When styling a bookcase on a budget, don't forget about your yard. Add pine cones to a display, stack wood slices for height on the shelves, or paint rocks with monograms to use as bookends. Even an over-sized stick can become a piece of art.

Begin your bookcase styling with a blank slate. Remove everything from your shelves. Next, stack books in the bookcase. (I know, right? Novel concept—books on a bookcase. Pun totally intended.) Place five to seven books on one side of one shelf and then five to seven books on the other side of the next shelf.

Leave space for your bookcase to breathe.

At the end of each row of books, occasionally turn two books on their sides and place a small accessory on top. Place decorative accessories in the blank spaces on the shelves where there aren't books. You can also place trays or baskets behind the books for additional height. Here are some unique ideas for bookcase accessories.

CREATE A LEAF WREATH

Think outside the bookcase with a simple wreath project. Start with a basic wire wreath form. Cut out between 45 to 50 leaf shapes from drop cloth (see page 137 for a template). Pinch the leaf at the end and glue the pinched ends together. Next, glue the pinched drop cloth leaf to the wire frame. Make sure you glue all the leaves in the same direction— clockwise or counter clockwise. Continue gluing until your wreath form is covered and then hang the wreath on the front of the bookcase.

BUILD A RECLAIMED WOOD FRAME

Everyone's picture looks cuter in a reclaimed wood frame. Cut six 1" x 2" x 8" pieces of wood. Lay four of the pieces of wood flat on a table side by side. Then, using wood glue, attach one of the two remaining pieces of wood to the top and one of the remaining pieces of wood to the bottom to hold the first four pieces of wood in place. Glue two tiny clothespins to the top piece of wood. Let the frame dry and then clip a picture into it.

MAKE YOUR OWN RECLAIMED WOOD MONOGRAM

Start with a 10" x 10" square of reclaimed wood (or even just wood that looks reclaimed if you squint). Find a plate to use as a template and trace around it with pencil. Next, trace a three-letter monogram inside the circle with carbon paper. Use a wood-stain pen to fill in the letters of the monogram and the outline of the circle.

Add personality to your
hutch with wood shims.
All you'll need is several
packages of wood shims
and wood glue. Begin by
staggering the wood shims in
a brick pattern on the back
of the hutch and then glue in
place. Then measure the end
pieces, mark on the shim with
a pencil, cut with scissors,
and glue in place. Seal the
wood, let dry, and go back to
styling your hutch.

Display Collections for an Authentic Hutch

A hutch is a great place to style collections. One of something is great, but add a few accessory friends, and it turns into something amazing.

The key to making a collection work is to style it in a similar color palette.

For example, mixing different styles of white dishes creates a harmonious display. Even if the dishes are different patterns, the overall color ties them together. Remember to display your collection in groups of three when displaying them on the hutch. Here are some creative ideas for unique hutch accessories.

EMBELLISH YOUR DISHES

Fill the shelves of your hutch with whiteware and thrift store dishes. And then? Take those dishes to the next level. Start with an oversized vinyl design from the craft store. The larger the better. Cut out pieces of the design and add sections of the vinyl design to individual plates. Once finished, all the plates work together to create the overall design.

PERSONALIZE A MINI PHOTO FRAME WREATH

If you are looking for ways to add personality to your hutch, why not create your own mini photo frame wreath? Fill tiny photo frames (from the wedding placeholder section of the craft store) with pictures. Then thread florist wire through the back of the photos and wire onto a grapevine wreath. Continue until your wreath is covered with frames and then hang it up on the front of the hutch.

MAKE YOUR OWN ACCESSORY

Did you know this book comes with its own DIY? One you can make in minutes? In the back (pages 139–143) are three free pieces of quote artwork painted especially for you. Simply tear out and put in a 5 x 7 frame for a unique accessory for your home or a gift for someone special.

Think Seasonal for a Fresh Mantel

Traditionally, mantels are the go-to choice for seasonal decorating. Christmas and Easter and spring and fall never met a mantel they didn't like. There are three important steps to mantel decorating: height, texture, and the rule of thirds. Start with height for the mantel by adding an oversized platter or basket.

Layer in pieces of different heights to break up the silhouette.

Next, add texture to the display. Shiny metallic accents or woven urns or distressed wood planters are all great options to add a little texture. Stick with odd numbers of items when arranging the display, and make sure to leave room for the eye to rest. Here are some ideas for unique mantel accessories.

CRAFT A NATURAL VASE

Shop your yard. Pick up some twigs. Select the cute ones. Bring them inside. Take a simple glass cylinder vase and glue the cute twigs around the circumference of it. Then fill the vase with flowers/leaves/branches from the yard.

ACCESSORIZE WITH A GARLAND

One fun way to accessorize your mantel is with a handmade garland. Make your own leather-and-felt garland in minutes (see page 137 for a template). Trace a basic leaf form onto felt. Repeat until you have about 40 leaves. Cut out the traced leaves and punch tiny holes at both ends of each of them. Thread leather cording through both ends of each of the leaves and continue until the entire piece of cording is covered. Tie off at the ends, arrange leaves evenly, and drape across the front of your mantel.

A Little Inspiration for the Road

- Always remember a frame (or a really pretty glass cloche) makes everything important. If you have something you want to showcase—such as a playbill or a wedding invitation or a runner's number—simply frame it, and it immediately becomes art.

- If one of something is good, three or more of that same something can be amazing. Even the simplest of objects becomes so much more when the rest of their family shows up for the reunion.

- Have fun. I once hung tiny chairs on a wall, and they were the talk of the county. Don't take your accessories too seriously. Your house will thank you.

Use baskets to organize

Create a coffee table display

Mix in natural elements

Create a coffee table from a dining table

Conclusion

Aren't you all about yourself now? You should be. You are a rock star. You've learned the principles of space planning. You've discovered how to select the perfect paint color for your space. You know enough about textiles and accessories and walls and windows and ceilings and moldings and mixing patterns to fill an entire set of encyclopedias.

And now? This isn't the end of your decorating journey—it's just the beginning. This planner is here to hold your hand and guide you on the decorating road ahead. Within these pages are the tools you need to plan rooms that are truly you and design warm and welcoming spaces for your house. There are pages and pages of inspiration to help create a home you truly love.

Oh...the rooms you will decorate.

Now comes the challenge—applying what you've learned. It's scary. I get it. If anyone understands, it's me. Decorating is full of choices, and sometimes it all seems so overwhelming. You might be worried you'll make a mistake. You might be worried it won't look right. You might be worried someone else won't like your choices.

Don't. Worry, that is.

Truth? God created us all to be unique. You were designed by an amazing, incredible, awe-inspiring Creator. In this entire world, there is no one else quite like you. You have your own style. You have your own likes and dislikes. You have your own individual perspective.

Let your home reflect *you*.

Now go forth and take on that shag carpet. Take on that pink-and-orange floral wallpaper. Take on the bookshelves in the living room and the chairs in the study. Take on those outdated countertops and that kitchen time has forgotten. And remember—your new home design is around the corner...

...just waiting for a rock star.

Check out the back of the book for some FUN EXTRAS to help you on your home decorating journey.

THE AUTHOR
KariAnne

KariAnne eats, sleeps, and breathes design. She calls herself the house whisperer for her uncanny talent in predicting someone's decor without ever seeing their house. She loves polka-dot patterns, DIY's, and Philippians 4:6-7. KariAnne's favorite room in her home is the kitchen—where all the stories come to eat lunch. And don't let her red lipstick fool you—her favorite color is actually gray.

THE ARTIST
Michal

A self-described rose-colored-glass-half-full optimist, Michal shares her life through her brushes, paints, and pencils. An artistic chameleon, Michal's creative interests are as varied as her taste in colors (favorites include orange, usually blue, but sometimes green), love of patterns (stripes especially), and music (pop, rock, classical, and even grunge). She once painted a room a vibrant lime green to let the outside in. Oops! Even artists make a color faux pas sometimes.

Resource Guide

SPACE PLANNING
Page 14
Sign (top left): Kirkland's
Pillow (top left): Kirkland's
Throw (top left): IKEA
Chandelier (top right): Painted Fox Home
Seagrass rug (bottom): Home
    Decorators Collection, Home Depot
Blue-and-white rug (bottom): Wayfair
Page 15
Wall color: Sherwin-Williams Mindful
    Gray SW 7016
Ottoman: Lamps Plus
Chair (left): Painted Fox Home
Chair (right): La-Z-Boy
Large textured pillows: HomeGoods

PAINT COLORS
Page 30
Wall color: Sherwin-Williams Coral
    Reef SW 6606
Table: IKEA
Organizer: IKEA
Polka-dot baskets: Hobby Lobby
Elephant sign: Hobby Lobby
Side table: Hobby Lobby
X bookshelf: IKEA
Lamp: Lamps Plus
Page 31
Wall color: Sherwin-Williams Repose
    Gray SW 7015
Blue-and-white rug: Birch Lane
USA wood sign: Hobby Lobby
Plaid throw: Birch Lane
Snowflake pillows: Birch Lane
Chair: Hobby Lobby
Basket: Birch Lane
Striped duvet: Birch Lane

FLOORING OPTIONS
Page 46
White stool (top left): IKEA
Page 47
Lamps: Lamps Plus
Sign: Painted Fox Home
Wood ampersand: Etsy Shop, SonofWhale
Desk organizer: Hobby Lobby

WALL TREATMENTS
Page 67
Wall stripe paint color: Sherwin-
    Williams Repose Gray SW 7015
Chandelier: Painted Fox Home
FARM letters: Etsy Shop, SonofWhale
Rug: Home Decorators Collection,
    Home Depot

WINDOW TREATMENTS
Page 82
Wall color (top right): Sherwin-Williams
    Rice Grain SW 6155
Page 83
Wall color: Sherwin-Williams
    Anonymous SW 7046
Smocked burlap curtains: Painted
    Fox Home

LIGHTING GUIDE
Page 94
Wall color (top left) Sherwin-Williams
    Rice Grain SW 6155
Lamp (top right): Lamps Plus
Chandelier (bottom): Painted Fox Home
Page 95
Rug: Home Decorators Collection,
    Home Depot
Kitchen island: IKEA
Metal bookshelf: Painted Fox Home
Oversized clock: Kirkland's
White dishes: Kirkland's
Metal drying rack: Painted Fox Home

PATTERN MIXING
Page 104
Farmhouse bedding (top left): IKEA
Rag pillow (top right): Better Homes
    and Gardens Collection, Walmart
Khaki-and-white pillow (bottom):
    Hobby Lobby
Page 105
Flower color 1: Sherwin-Williams
    Sockeye SW 6619
Flower color 2: Sherwin-Williams
    Rejuvenate SW 6620
Flower color 3: Sherwin-Williams
    Habanero Chile SW 7589

ACCESSORY STYLING
Page 122
Metal spheres (top left): Hobby Lobby
Baskets (top right): Kirkland's
Wood ampersand (bottom): Etsy Shop,
    SonofWhale
Page 123
Rug: Home Decorators Collection,
    Home Depot
Basket: Birch Lane
Rattan chairs: Home Depot

Visit these retailers online!
www.birchlane.com
www.etsy.com/people/sonofwhale
www.hobbylobby.com
www.homedepot.com
www.homegoods.com
www.ikea.com
www.kirklands.com
www.lampsplus.com
www.la-z-boy.com
www.natman.com
www.paintedfoxhome.com
www.sherwin-williams.com
www.walmart.com
www.wayfair.com

COMING SOON
from KariAnne

But Where Do I Put the Couch?
And Answers to 100 Other Home Decorating Questions

KariAnne teams up with Melissa Michaels (bestselling author and creator of
the award-winning blog, The Inspired Room) to tackle your toughest and most asked
decorating questions. Get the answers you need to overcome your biggest decorating
challenges from two home decor bloggers that have been there and done that.

What's Your Decorating Style?

After taking the What's Your Decorating Style Quiz to determine which one of
five basic styles best fits you, get fantastic decorating tips for each part of your house.
From the front entry to the back porch and every room in between, KariAnne will
help you create a consistent decorating theme throughout your home,
one that truly reflects your personal style.

Join KariAnne in celebrating the incredible, awesome, special individual that is within each of us!

so close to amazing

Stories of a DIY life gone wrong . . .
and learning to find the beauty
in every imperfection

KariAnne Wood
Author of the Thistlewood Farms blog

1

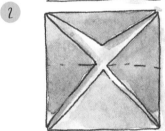

2

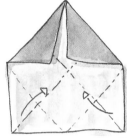

MAKE YOUR OWN
Origami Bookmark

1. Cut a piece of paper into a 7 x 7-inch square and a 2 x 7-inch rectangle. (Set aside the rectangle for now.) Fold the square across both diagonals.

2. Using the square piece of paper, fold all four corners into the middle of the "X" you just made.

3. Flip the square over, and fold the four corners in again. Repeat once more. (Your flower should be about 2 inches square now.)

4. Fold each triangle tip outward so that half of it sticks out beyond the square.

5. Flip over and fold each of the inner flaps outward. The flower is now done!

3

5

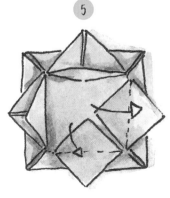

FINISHED!

4

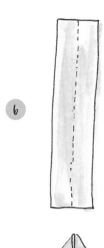

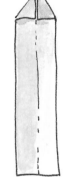

6. Now, using the rectangular piece, crease it in half, vertically.

7. Fold in the top two corners to the middle line.

8. Fold the rectangle in half, horizontally.

9. Diagonally crease the paper going through the midline crease you just made, making an "X".

10. Pinch the two sides together that were created by the creases you just made. (They should fold inward, and the top half should meet the bottom.)

11. Lock the hexagon you just made into the back of the flower. (The two corners should slide perfectly into the folds on the back of the flower.)

12. Flip over. The bookmark is complete—you can slide it onto the page to mark your spot!

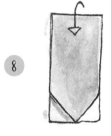

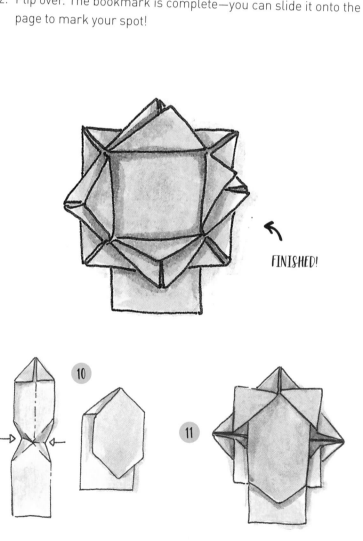

FINISHED!

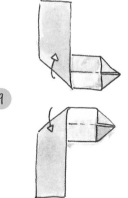

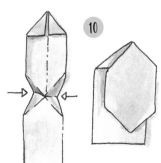

Color Wheel

REMOVE FROM BOOK FOR REFERENCE

STEPS TO CREATE A COLOR PALETTE

1. Start with a color you love.
2. Are you more drawn to its neighbors or the contrasting color?
3. From there, determine your dominant color, secondary color, and an accent color. (Don't forget the power of a good neutral!).

Kitchen

Bathroom

USE ON PAGES 108-109

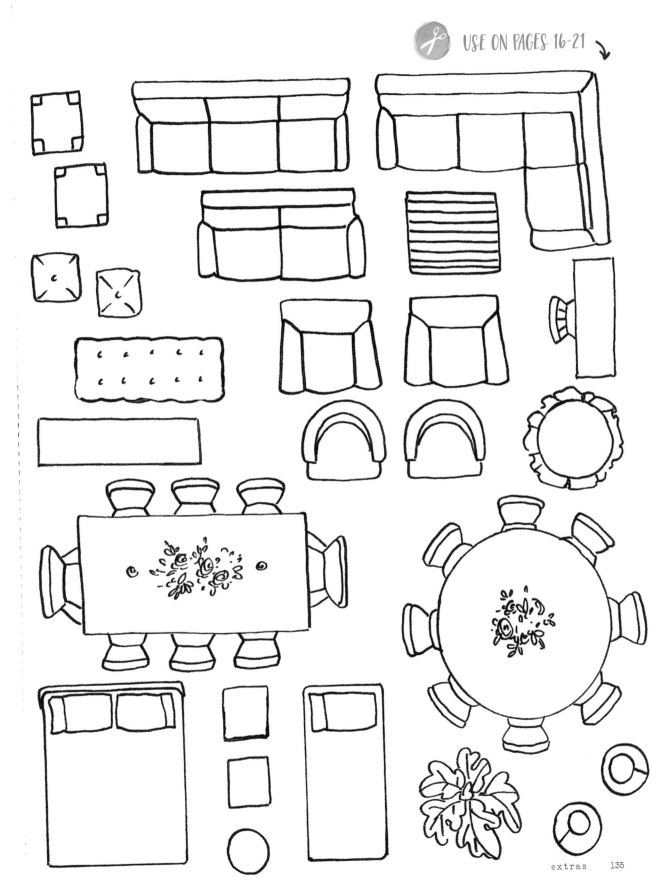

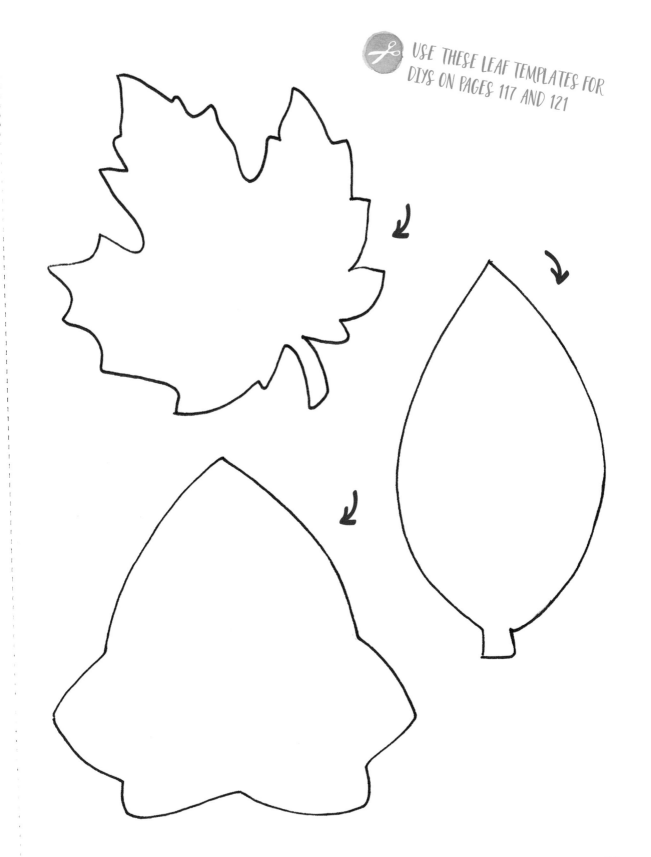

In this entire world there is no one else quite like you